# Contents

# ASP.NET MVC Framework Preview

by Steven Sanderson

ASP.NET MVC is a new web development framework from Microsoft that combines the effectiveness and tidiness of model-view-controller (MVC) architecture, the most up-to-date ideas and techniques from agile development, and the best parts of the existing ASP.NET platform. It's a complete alternative to the WebForms platform, delivering considerable advantages for all but the most trivial of web development projects.

In this short book, you'll learn about the reasons why ASP.NET MVC exists, how it's different from other Microsoft web development platforms, and what benefits you might get from using it. After that, you'll find a tutorial on building a simple data entry application, illustrating many of the facilities and techniques that are important in ASP.NET MVC. Finally, you'll learn about the architectural and design principles that underlie ASP.NET MVC, including MVC architecture, component-oriented design, and testability.

At the time of writing, the most up-to-date public release of ASP.NET MVC is Preview 4 (i.e., the fourth CTP release). Microsoft has indicated that the full and final v1 release should be available before the end of 2008. You can expect various aspects of the software to change between now and then, which is why this book doesn't dwell on documenting the API in detail, but rather focuses on the underlying principles. When ASP.NET MVC reaches its final release, look out for *Pro ASP.NET MVC Framework* (part of the Apress Pro series), by the same author, which will be a thorough guide to using every aspect of ASP.NET MVC.

# Chapter 1: What's the Big Idea

To understand the distinctive aspects and design goals of ASP.NET MVC, it's worth considering the history of web development so far—brief though it may be. Among Microsoft's web development platforms, we've seen over the years an ongoing increase in power and (unfortunately) complexity. As shown in Table 1-1, each new platform tackled the specific shortcomings of its predecessor.

In just the same way, ASP.NET MVC is designed to tackle the specific shortcomings of traditional ASP.NET WebForms, but this time by trying to emphasize simplicity.

*Table 1-1. Microsoft's Lineage of Web Development Technologies*

| TIME PERIOD | TECHNOLOGY | STRENGTHS | WEAKNESSES |
|---|---|---|---|
| Jurassic | Common Gateway Interface (CGI)* | Simple<br>Flexible<br>Only option at the time | Runs outside web server, so is resource intensive (spawns separate OS process per request)<br>Low-level |

*Table 1-1. (continued)*

| TIME PERIOD | TECHNOLOGY | STRENGTHS | WEAKNESSES |
|---|---|---|---|
| Bronze age | Microsoft Internet Database Connector (IDC) | Runs inside web server | Just a wrapper for SQL queries and templates for formatting result set |
| 1996 | Active Server Pages (ASP) | General purpose | Interpreted at runtime<br><br>Encouraged "spaghetti code" |
| 2002/03 | ASP.NET 1.0/1.1 | Compiled "Stateful" UI<br><br>Vast infrastructure<br><br>Encourages object-oriented programming | Heavy on bandwidth<br><br>Ugly HTML<br><br>Untestable |
| 2005 | ASP.NET 2.0 | | |
| 2007 | ASP.NET AJAX | | |
| 2008 | ASP.NET 3.5 | | |

\* CGI is a standard means of of connecting a web server to an arbitrary executable program that returns dynamic content. Specification maintained by National Center for Supercomputing Applications (NCSA).

# Traditional ASP.NET

ASP.NET was a huge shift when it first arrived, not just in terms of the brand-new .NET multilanguage managed code platform (which was a landmark in its own right), but in that it sought to close the gap between stateful, object-oriented Windows Forms development and stateless, HTML-oriented web development.

Microsoft attempted to hide both HTTP (with its intrinsic statelessness) and HTML (which, at the time, was unfamiliar to many developers) by modeling a user interface (UI) as a server-side hierarchy of control objects.

Each control kept track of its own state across requests (using the ViewState facility), automatically rendered itself as HTML when needed, and automatically connected client-side events (e.g., a button click) with the corresponding server-side event handler code. In effect, WebForms is a giant abstraction layer aimed to deliver a classic event-driven GUI over the Web.

Developers no longer had to work with a series of independent HTTP requests and responses, as we did with earlier technologies; we could now think in terms of a stateful UI. We could "forget" about the Web, build UIs using a drag-and-drop designer, and imagine that everything happened on the server.

## What's Wrong with Traditional ASP.NET?

Traditional ASP.NET was a fine idea, and a thrilling prospect at first, but of course reality turned out to be more complicated. Over the years, real-world use of WebForms uncovered a range of weaknesses:

*ViewState*: The actual mechanism of maintaining state across requests (ViewState) often results in giant blocks of data being transferred between client and server. It can reach hundreds of kilobytes in many real-world applications, and it goes back and forth with *every* request, frustrating site visitors with a long wait each time they click a button or try to move to the next page on a grid. ASP.NET AJAX suffers this just as badly,[1] even though bandwidth-heavy page updating is one of the main problems that Ajax is supposed to solve.

*Page life cycle*: The mechanism of connecting client-side events with server-side event handler code, part of the page life cycle, can be extraordinarily complicated and delicate. Few developers have success manipulating the control hierarchy at runtime without getting ViewState errors or finding that some event handlers mysteriously fail to execute.

---

[1] It has to send the entire page's ViewState data back and forth in each asynchronous request.

***Limited control over HTML***: Server controls render themselves as HTML, but not necessarily the HTML you want. Not only does their HTML often fail to comply with web standards or make good use of CSS, but the system of server controls generates unpredictable and complex ID values, which are hard to access using JavaScript.

***False sense of separation of concerns***: ASP.NET's *code-behind* model provides a means to take application code out of its HTML markup and into a separate code-behind class. This has been widely applauded for separating logic and presentation, but in reality, developers are encouraged to mix presentation code (e.g., manipulating the server-side control tree) with application logic (e.g., manipulating database data) in these same monstrous code-behind classes. Without better separation of concerns, the end result is often fragile and unintelligible.

***Untestable***: When ASP.NET's designers first set out their platform, they could not have anticipated that automated testing would become such a mainstream part of software development as it is today. Not surprisingly, the architecture they designed is totally unsuitable for automated testing.

ASP.NET has kept moving. Version 2.0 added a set of standard application components that can significantly reduce the amount of code you need to write yourself. The AJAX release in 2007 was Microsoft's response to the Web 2.0/Ajax frenzy of the day, supporting rich client-side interactivity while keeping developers' lives simple.[2] The most recent 3.5 release is a smaller enhancement, adding support for .NET 3.5 features and a set of new controls. The new ASP.NET *Dynamic Data* facility generates simple database list/edit screens automatically.

---

[2] Ironically, Microsoft actually invented `XMLHttpRequest`, the backbone of Ajax technology, to support Outlook Web Access. However, Microsoft didn't really capitalize on its potential until hundreds of others already had.

# Web Development Today

Outside Microsoft, web development technology has been progressing rapidly in several different directions. Aside from Ajax, which I've already noted, there have been a few other major developments.

## Web Standards and REST

The drive for web standards compliance hasn't reduced in recent years; if anything, it's increased. Web sites are consumed on a greater variety of devices and browsers than ever before, and web standards (for HTML, CSS, JavaScript, etc.) remain our one great hope for getting a decent browsing experience everywhere (even on the Internet-enabled refrigerator). Modern web platforms cannot afford to ignore the business case and the weight of developer enthusiasm for web standards compliance.

At the same time, REST[3] is gaining enormous popularity as an architecture for application interoperability over HTTP—especially in the Web 2.0 world of informal "mash-ups." The distinction between web services and web applications is eroding now that we have rich Ajax and Silverlight clients, and REST dominates over SOAP in these scenarios. REST requires an approach to HTTP and URL handling that is not easily supported by traditional ASP.NET.

## Agile and Test-Driven Development

It's not just web development that's moved on in the last decade—software development as a whole has experienced a shift toward *agile* methodologies. This means a lot of different things to different people, but

---

[3] *Representational State Transfer* describes an application in terms of resources (URIs) representing real-world entities and standard operations (HTTP methods) representing available operations on those resources. For example, you might PUT a new `http://www.example.com/Products/Lawnmower` or DELETE `http://www.example.com/Customers/Arnold-Smith`.

is largely about running software projects as adaptable processes of discovery, resisting the encumbrance of excessive bureaucracy and restrictive forward planning. Enthusiasm for agile methodologies tends to go hand in hand with enthusiasm for a particular set of development practices and tools—usually open source—that promote and assist such practices.

*Test-driven development (TDD)* is the obvious example, in which developers increase their ability to respond to change without compromising the stability of their code base, because each known and desired behavior is already codified in a suite of tens, hundreds, or thousands of automated tests that can be verified at any moment. There's no shortage of .NET tools to support automated testing, but they can only be applied effectively to software that's designed as a set of cleanly separated, independent modules. Unfortunately, you cannot describe typical WebForms applications in that way.

The .NET open source and independent software vendor (ISV) community has produced no end of top-quality unit testing frameworks (NUnit, MBUnit), mocking frameworks (Rhino Mocks, Moq), inversion-of-control containers (Castle Windsor, Spring.NET), continuous integration servers (Cruise Control, TeamCity), object-relational mappers (NHibernate, Subsonic), and the like, and proponents of these tools and techniques have even found a common voice, publishing and organizing conferences under the shared brand ALT.NET. Traditional ASP.NET WebForms is not very amenable to these tools and techniques because of its monolithic design, so from this vocal group of experts and industry thought leaders, traditional ASP.NET WebForms gets little respect.

## Ruby on Rails

In 2004, Ruby on Rails was a quiet, open source contribution from an unknown player. Suddenly it hit fame, transforming the rules of web development. It's not so much that it contained revolutionary technology, but more that it took existing ingredients and blended them in such a wonderful, magical, delicious way as to put existing platforms to shame.

By applying MVC architecture (an old pattern that many web frameworks have recently rediscovered), by working in tune with the HTTP protocol instead of against it, by promoting conventions instead of the need for configuration, and by integrating an object-relational mapping (ORM) tool into its core, Rails applications more or less fell into place without much expense of effort. It was as if this was how web development should have been all along; as if we'd suddenly realized we'd been fighting our tools all these years, but now the war was over.

Rails shows that web standards compliance and RESTfulness don't have to be hard. It also shows that agile and test-driven development work best when the framework is designed to support them. The rest of the web development world has been catching up ever since.

## Key Benefits of ASP.NET MVC

A huge corporation like Microsoft can afford to rest on its laurels for a while, but not forever. ASP.NET has been a great commercial success so far, but as discussed, the rest of the web development world has moved on, and even though Microsoft has kept dusting the cobwebs off WebForms, its essential design has started to look quite antiquated.

In October 2007, at the very first ALT.NET conference in Austin, Texas, Microsoft general manager Scott Guthrie announced and demonstrated a brand-new MVC web development platform, built on ASP.NET, clearly designed as a direct response to the criticisms laid out previously. The following sections describe how it overcomes ASP.NET's limitations and brings Microsoft's platform back to the cutting edge.

# Model-View-Controller Architecture

ASP.NET MVC provides greatly improved separation of concerns thanks to its adoption of MVC architecture. The MVC pattern isn't new—it dates back to 1978 and the Smalltalk project at Xerox PARC—but it's gaining enormous popularity today as an architecture for web applications, perhaps because of the following:

- User interaction with an MVC application naturally follows a cycle: the user takes an action, and then in response the application changes its data model and delivers an updated view to the user. And then the cycle repeats. This is a very convenient fit for web applications delivered as a series of HTTP requests and responses.

- Web applications already necessitate combining several technologies (e.g., databases, HTML, and executable code), usually split into a set of tiers or layers, and the patterns that arise naturally map onto the concepts in MVC.

ASP.NET MVC implements a modern variant on MVC that's especially suitable for web applications. You'll learn more about the theory and practice of this architecture in Chapter 3.

Through this design, ASP.NET MVC directly answers the competition of Ruby on Rails and similar platforms, making a serious effort to bring this style of development into the mainstream of the .NET world, capitalizing on the experience and best practices discovered by developers using other platforms, and in some ways pushing forward beyond what even Rails can offer.

## Extensibility

Your desktop PC's internal components are independent pieces that interact only across standard, publicly documented interfaces, so you can easily take out your graphics card or hard disk and replace it with another one from a different manufacturer, confident that it will slot in and work. In just the same way, the MVC Framework is built as a series of independent components—satisfying a .NET interface or built on an abstract base class—so you can easily replace the routing system, the view engine, the controller factory, or any other framework component, with a different one of your own implementation. In fact, the framework's designers set out to give you three options for each MVC Framework component:

1. Use the *default* implementation of the component as it stands (which should be enough for most applications).

2. Derive a *subclass* of the default implementation to tweak its behavior.

3. *Replace* the component entirely with a new implementation of the interface or abstract base class.

It's like the Provider model from ASP.NET 2.0, but taken much further—right into the heart of the MVC Framework.

## Testability

MVC architecture gives you a great start in making your application maintainable and testable, because you will naturally separate different application concerns into different, independent software pieces.

Yet the ASP.NET MVC designers didn't stop there. They took the framework's component-oriented design and made sure each separate piece was ideally structured for automated testing. So, you can write clean, simple unit tests for each controller and action in your application, using fake or mock implementations of framework components to simulate any scenario. The framework's design works around the limitations of today's testing and mocking tools, and adds Visual Studio wizards to create starter test projects on your behalf (integrating with open source unit test tools such as NUnit and MBUnit as well as Microsoft's MSTest), so even if you've never written a unit test before, you'll be off to a great start. Welcome to the world of maintainable code!

Throughout this book, you'll see examples of how to write automated tests using a variety of testing and mocking strategies.

## Tight Control over HTML

The MVC Framework recognizes the importance of producing clean, standards-compliant markup. Its built-in HTML helper methods do of course produce XHTML-compliant output, but there's a bigger change of mindset at work. Instead of spewing out huge swathes of barely readable HTML code to represent what should be simple UI elements like lists, tables, or string literals, the MVC Framework encourages you to craft simple, elegant markup styled with CSS. (Plus, Visual Studio 2008's massively improved CSS refactoring support finally makes it possible to keep track of and sensibly reuse your CSS rules no matter how big your project gets.)

Of course, if you do want to throw in some ready-made widgets for complex UI elements like date pickers or cascading menus, ASP.NET MVC's "no special requirements" approach to markup makes it dead easy to use best-of-breed open source UI libraries such as jQuery or the Yahoo UI Library to accomplish rich, cross-browser interactivity with a minimum of fuss (along with all the obligatory Ajax goodness).

ASP.NET MVC–generated pages don't contain any ViewState data, so they can be hundreds of kilobytes smaller than typical pages from ASP.NET WebForms. Despite today's fast broadband connections, this bandwidth saving still gives an enormously improved end user experience.

## Powerful New Routing System

Today's web developers recognize the importance of using clean URLs. It isn't good for business to use incomprehensible URLs like `/App_v2/User/Page.aspx?action=show%20prop&prop_id=82742`—it's far more professional to use `/to-rent/chicago/2303-silver-street`.

Why does it matter? Firstly, search engines give considerable weight to keywords found in a URL. A search for "rent in chicago" is much more likely to turn up the latter URL. Secondly, many web users are now savvy enough to understand a URL, and appreciate the option of navigating by typing into their browser's address bar. Thirdly, when someone feels they can understand a URL, they're more likely to link to it (being confident that it doesn't expose any of their own personal information) or share it with a friend (perhaps reading it out over the phone). Fourthly, it doesn't pointlessly expose the technical details, folder, and file name structure of your application with the whole public Internet (so you're free to change the underlying implementation without breaking all your incoming links).

Clean URLs were hard to implement in earlier frameworks, but ASP.NET MVC uses the brand-new `System.Web.Routing` facility to give you clean URLs by default. This gives you total control over your URL schema and its mapping to your controllers and actions, with no need to conform to any predefined pattern. Of course, this means you can easily define a modern REST-style URL schema if you're so inclined.

## Built on the Best Parts of the ASP.NET Platform

Microsoft's existing platform provides a mature, well-proven suite of components and facilities that can cut down your workload and increase your freedom. Firstly and most obviously, since ASP.NET MVC is based on the .NET 3.5 platform, you have the flexibility to write code in any .NET language[4] and access the same API features, not just in MVC itself, but in the extensive .NET class library and the vast ecosystem of third-party .NET libraries.

Secondly, ready-made ASP.NET platform features such as master pages, forms authentication, membership, roles, profiles, and globalization can significantly reduce the amount of code you need to develop and maintain in any web application, and these are just as effective in an MVC project as in a classic WebForms project. Many of WebForms' built-in server

---

[4] You can even build ASP.NET MVC applications in IronRuby or IronPython, although most businesses are likely to stick with C# and Visual Basic for the time being. This book focuses exclusively on C#.

controls—and your own custom controls from earlier ASP.NET projects—can be reused in an ASP.NET MVC application (as long as they don't depend on WebForms-specific notions such as ViewState).

Development and deployment are covered, too. Not only is ASP.NET well integrated into Visual Studio, Microsoft's flagship commercial IDE, it's *the* native web programming technology supported by the IIS web server built into Windows XP, Vista, and Server products. IIS 7.0 adds a set of enhanced features for running .NET managed code as part of the request handling pipeline, giving special treatment to ASP.NET applications. Being built on the core ASP.NET platform, MVC applications get an equal share of the benefits.

## .NET 3.5 Language Innovations

Since its inception in 2002, Microsoft's .NET platform has evolved relentlessly, supporting and even defining the state-of-the-art aspects of modern programming. The most significant recent innovation is *Language Integrated Query (LINQ)*, along with bucketloads of ancillary enhancements in C# such as lambda expressions and anonymous typing. ASP.NET MVC is designed with these innovations in mind, so many of its API methods and coding patterns follow a cleaner, more expressive composition than was possible when earlier platforms were invented.

## Get the Source Code

Faced with competition from open source alternatives, Microsoft has made a brave new move with ASP.NET MVC. Unlike with any previous Microsoft web development platform, you're free to download the original source code to ASP.NET MVC, and even modify and compile your own version of it. This is invaluable for those occasions when your debugging trail leads into a system component and you want to step into its code (even reading the original programmers' comments), and also if you're building an advanced component and want to see what development possibilities exist, or how the built-in components actually work.

Of course, this ability is also great if you don't like the way something works, find a bug, or just want to access something that's otherwise inaccessible, because you can simply change it yourself. However, you'll need to keep track of your changes and reapply them if you upgrade to a newer version of the framework. Source control is your friend here.

Don't be mistaken, though: ASP.NET MVC is *not* an open source project. Nobody outside Microsoft is allowed to submit their changes back to the central, official build. If you tweak the framework for your own benefit, that's fine, and you're free to deploy it to your production web servers, but Microsoft will only ship code that's the product of their own development and QA teams.

You can browse and download the framework's source code at `www.codeplex.com/aspnet`.

# Who Should Use ASP.NET MVC?

As with any new technology, its mere existence isn't a good reason for adopting it (despite the natural tendencies of we developers). Let's consider how the MVC platform compares to its most obvious alternatives.

## Comparisons with ASP.NET WebForms

You've already heard about the weaknesses and limitations in traditional ASP.NET WebForms, and how ASP.NET MVC overcomes many of those problems. That doesn't mean that WebForms is dead, though: Microsoft is keen to remind everyone that the two platforms go forward side by side, equally supported, and both are subject to active, ongoing development. In many ways, your choice between the two is a matter of development philosophy.

- WebForms takes the view that UIs should be *stateful*, and to that end adds a sophisticated abstraction layer on top of HTTP and HTML, using ViewState and postbacks to create the effect of statefulness. This makes it suitable for drag-and-drop Windows Forms–style development, in which you pull UI widgets onto a canvas and fill in code for their event handlers.

- MVC embraces HTTP's true stateless nature, working with it rather than fighting against it. It requires you to understand how web applications actually work; but given that understanding, it provides a simple, powerful, and modern approach to writing web applications with tidy code that's easy to test and maintain over time, free of bizarre complications and painful limitations.

There are certainly cases where WebForms is at least as good as, and probably better than, MVC. The obvious example is small, intranet-type applications that are largely about binding grids directly to database tables or stepping users through a wizard. Since you don't need to worry about the bandwidth issues that come with ViewState, don't need to be concerned with search engine optimization, and aren't bothered about testability or long-term maintenance, WebForms' drag-and-drop development strengths outweigh its weaknesses.

On the other hand, if you're writing applications for the public Internet, or larger intranet applications (e.g., more than a few person-month's work), you'll be aiming for fast download speeds and cross-browser compatibility, built with higher-quality, well-architected code suitable for automated testing, in which case MVC will deliver significant advantages for you.

## Migrating from WebForms to MVC

If you have an ongoing ASP.NET project that you're considering migrating to MVC, you'll be pleased to know that the two technologies can coexist in the same application at the same time. This gives you an opportunity to migrate your application piecemeal, especially if it's already partitioned into layers with your domain model or business logic held separately to the

WebForms pages. In some cases, you might even deliberately design an application to be a hybrid of the two approaches.

## Comparisons with Ruby on Rails

Rails has become a bit of a benchmark against which other web platforms must be compared. In this case, the simple reality is that developers and companies who are in the Microsoft .NET world will find ASP.NET MVC far easier to adopt and to learn, whereas developers and companies that work in Python or Ruby on Linux or Mac OS X will find an easier path into Rails. It's unlikely that you'd migrate from Rails to ASP.NET MVC or vice versa. There are some real differences in scope between the two technologies, though.

Rails is a completely *holistic* development platform, meaning that it handles the entire stack, right from database source control (migrations), through ORM, into handling requests with controllers and actions and writing automated tests, all topped off with a "scaffolding" system for rapidly creating data-oriented applications.

ASP.NET MVC, on the other hand, focuses purely on the task of handling web requests in MVC style with controllers and actions. It does not have a built-in ORM tool, nor a built-in unit testing tool, nor a system for managing database migrations, and not even a scaffolding system, because the .NET platform already has an enormous range of choices, and you should be able to use any one of them. For example, if you're looking for an ORM tool, you might use NHibernate, or Microsoft's LINQ to SQL, or Subsonic, or one of the many other mature solutions. Such is the luxury of the .NET platform, although of course it means that these components can't be as tightly integrated into ASP.NET MVC as the equivalents are into Rails.

## Comparisons with MonoRail

Up until now, the leading .NET MVC web development platform had been Castle MonoRail, which is part of the open source Castle project in development since 2003. If you know MonoRail, you'll find ASP.NET MVC uncannily familiar: they're both based on the core ASP.NET platform and they're both heavily inspired by Ruby on Rails. They use the same terminology in various places (MonoRail's founder has been involved in Microsoft's design process for ASP.NET MVC), and tend to attract the same kind of developers. There are differences, though:

- MonoRail can run on ASP.NET 2.0, whereas ASP.NET MVC requires version 3.5.

- Unlike ASP.NET MVC, MonoRail gives special treatment to one particular ORM. If you use Castle ActiveRecord (which is based on NHibernate), MonoRail can generate basic data-browsing and data entry UIs automatically (i.e., scaffolding).

- MonoRail is even more similar to Ruby on Rails. As well as using Rails-like terminology in places (flash, rescues, layouts, etc.), it has a more rigid sense of design by convention. MonoRail applications tend to use the same standard URL schema (`/controller/action`).

- MonoRail doesn't have a direct equivalent to ASP.NET MVC's routing system. The only way to accept nonstandard inbound URL patterns is to use a URL rewriting system, and if you do that, there isn't a tidy way to generate outbound URLs. (It's likely that MonoRail users will find a way to use the new `System.Web.Routing` to share the benefits.)

Both platforms have their pros and cons, but ASP.NET MVC has one giant advantage that guarantees it will enjoy far wider acceptance: the Microsoft badge. Whether you like it or not, this really matters in many practical scenarios of trying to convince a client or boss to accept a new technology. Plus, when the elephant moves, swarms of flies follow: thousands of developers, bloggers, and third-party component vendors (and authors!) are scrambling to claim the best places in the new ASP.NET MVC world, making support, tools, and staff far easier to find than—sadly—could ever be possible for MonoRail.

## Summary

In this chapter, you've seen how web development has evolved at tremendous speed from the primordial swamp of CGI executables to the latest high-performance, agile-compliant platforms. You reviewed the strengths, weaknesses, and limitations of ASP.NET WebForms, Microsoft's main web platform since 2002, and the changes in the wider web development industry that forced Microsoft to respond with something new.

You've seen how this new ASP.NET MVC platform directly addresses the criticisms leveled at ASP.NET WebForms, and how its modern design delivers enormous advantages to developers who are willing to understand HTTP, and who want to write high-quality, maintainable code. You've also seen how this platform leads to faster-performing applications that work better on a wider range of devices.

In the next chapter, you'll see the code in action, learning the simple mechanisms that yield all these benefits.

# Chapter 2: Your First ASP.NET MVC Application

The best way to appreciate a software development framework is to jump right in and use it. In this chapter, you'll create a simple data entry application using the ASP.NET MVC Framework.

---

**Note**     In this chapter, the pace is deliberately slow. For example, you'll be given step-by-step instructions on how to complete even small tasks such as adding new files to your project.

---

## Preparing Your Workstation

To get started with ASP.NET MVC development, you need to install to your workstation:

- Visual Studio 2008 (Standard, Professional, or Team System editions)[5]

- The ASP.NET MVC Framework

At the time of writing, the latest version of ASP.NET MVC is Preview 4, which you can obtain from Microsoft's Codeplex site at `http://tinyurl.com/mvc-p4`.[6] Download the runtime binary and install it.

Note that you can also get the framework's source code from the same page on Codeplex, and should have no trouble opening and building it in Visual Studio.

---

[5] You can also use the free Visual Web Developer 2008 Express Edition SP1, even though this book specifically refers to Visual Studio.

[6] This URL is an alias to `http://www.codeplex.com/aspnet/Release/ProjectReleases.aspx?ReleaseId=15389`.

# Creating a New ASP.NET MVC Project

Once you've installed the ASP.NET MVC Framework, you'll find that Visual Studio 2008 offers ASP.NET MVC Web Application as a new project type. To create a new ASP.NET MVC project, open Visual Studio and go to File ➤ New ➤ Project. Make sure the framework selector (top-right) reads .NET Framework 3.5, and select ASP.NET MVC Web Application, as shown in Figure 2-1.

*Figure 2-1. Creating a new ASP.NET MVC web application*

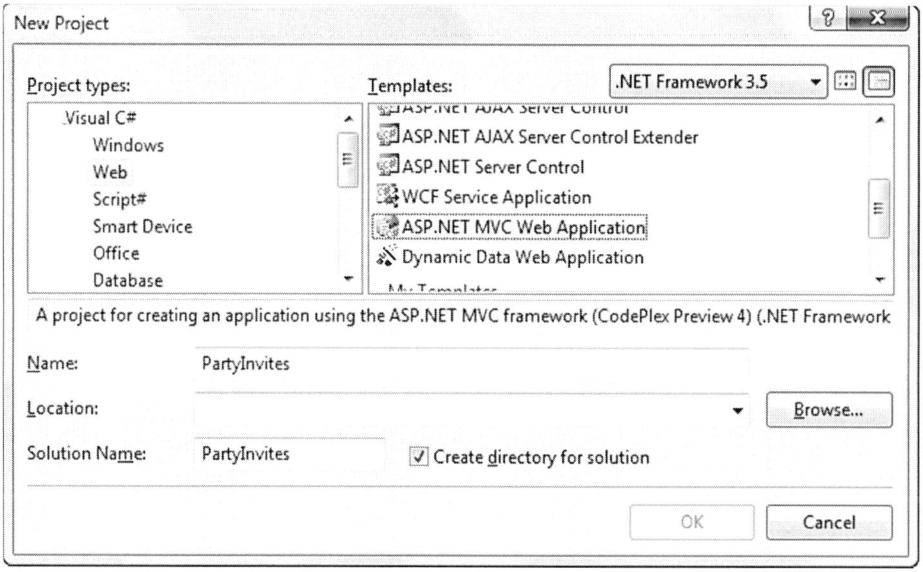

You can call your project anything you like, but since this demonstration application will handle RSVPs for a party (you'll hear more about that later), a good name would be PartyInvites.

When you click OK, the first thing you'll see is a pop-up window asking if you'd like to create a unit test project, as shown in Figure 2-2.

*Figure 2-2. Visual Studio prompts you to create a unit test project.*

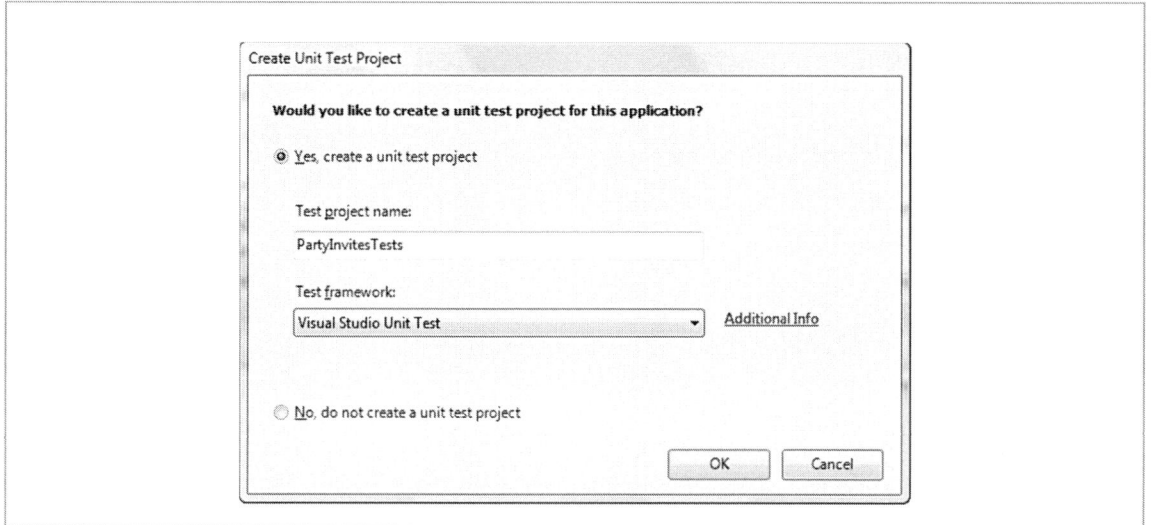

For simplicity, we won't write any unit tests for this application (though you will learn more about them in Chapter 3). You can choose "No, do not create a unit test project" (or you can choose Yes—it won't make any difference). Click OK.

## Removing Unnecessary Files

Visual Studio will now set up a default project structure for you. Helpfully, it adds a default "controller" and "view," so that you can just press F5 (or go to Debug ➤ Start Debugging) and immediately see something working. Try this now if you like (if it prompts you to enable debugging, just click OK) (see Figure 2-3).

*Figure 2-3. The default newborn ASP.NET MVC application*

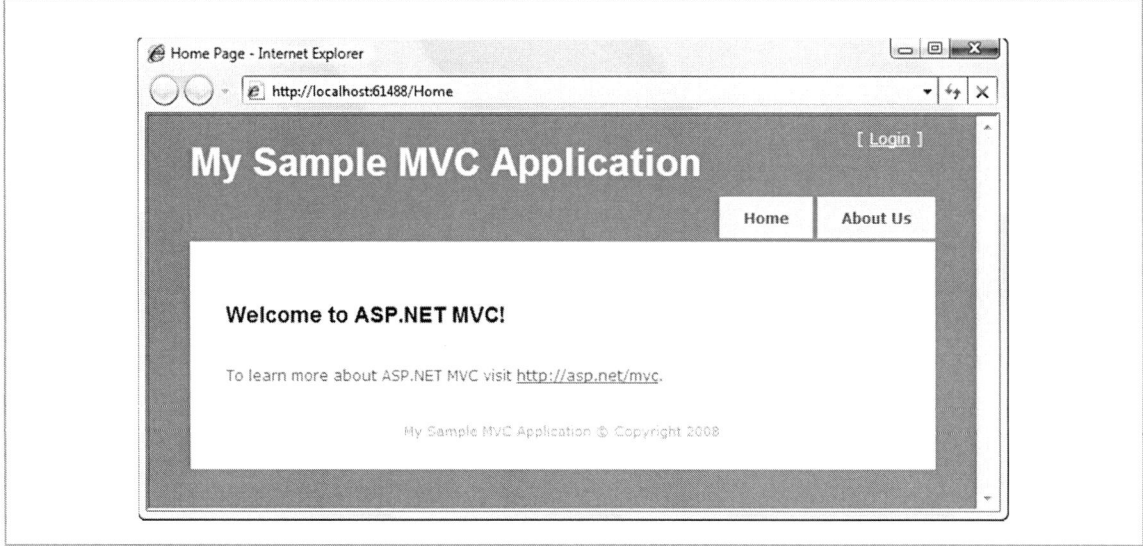

When you're done, be sure to stop debugging by closing any Internet Explorer window that appeared, or by going back to Visual Studio and pressing Shift+F5.

Unfortunately, in its quest to be helpful, Visual Studio goes a bit too far. It's already created for you a miniapplication skeleton, complete with user registration and authentication. That's a distraction from *really* understanding what's going on, so we're going to delete all that and get back to a blank canvas. Using Solution Explorer, delete each of the files and folders indicated in Figure 2-4 (right-click them, and then choose Delete).

*Figure 2-4. Pruning the default project template back to a sensible starting point*

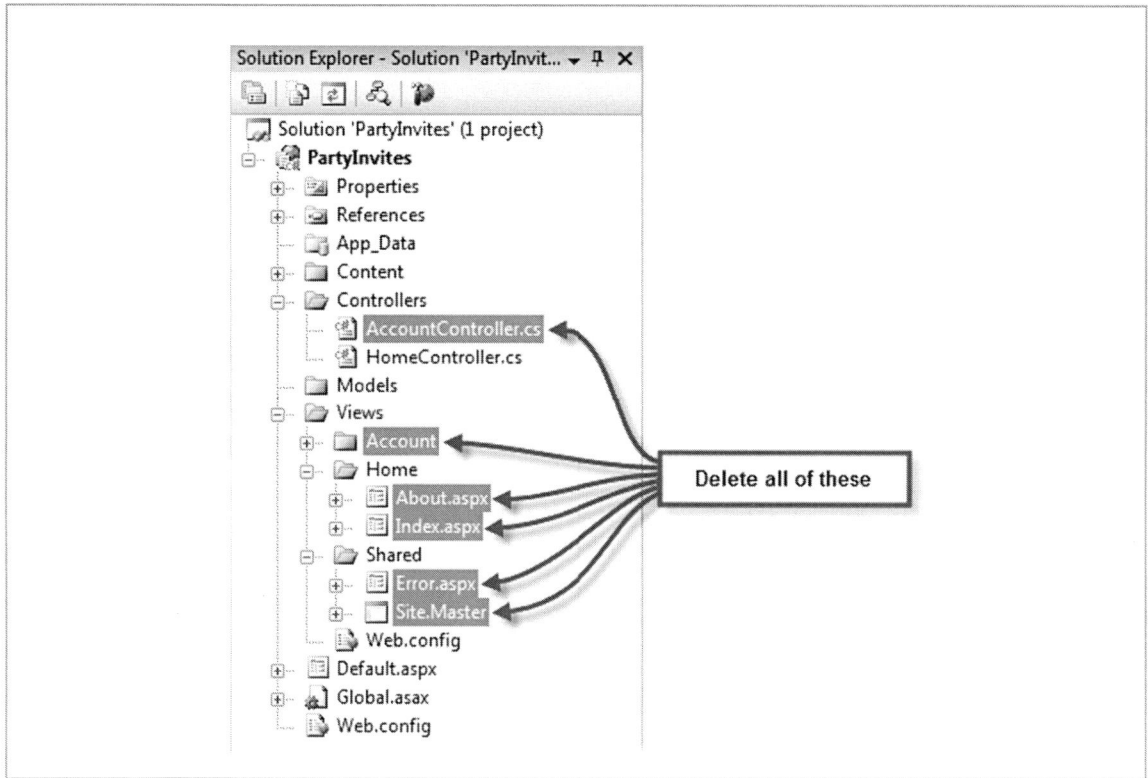

The last bit of tidying will be done inside HomeController.cs. Remove any code that's already there, and replace the whole HomeController class with this:

```
public class HomeController : Controller
{
    public string Index()
    {
        return "Hello, world!";
    }
}
```

It isn't very exciting—it's just a way of checking that your installation is working properly. Try running the project now (press F5), and you should see your message displayed in a browser, as in Figure 2-5.

*Figure 2-5. The initial application output*

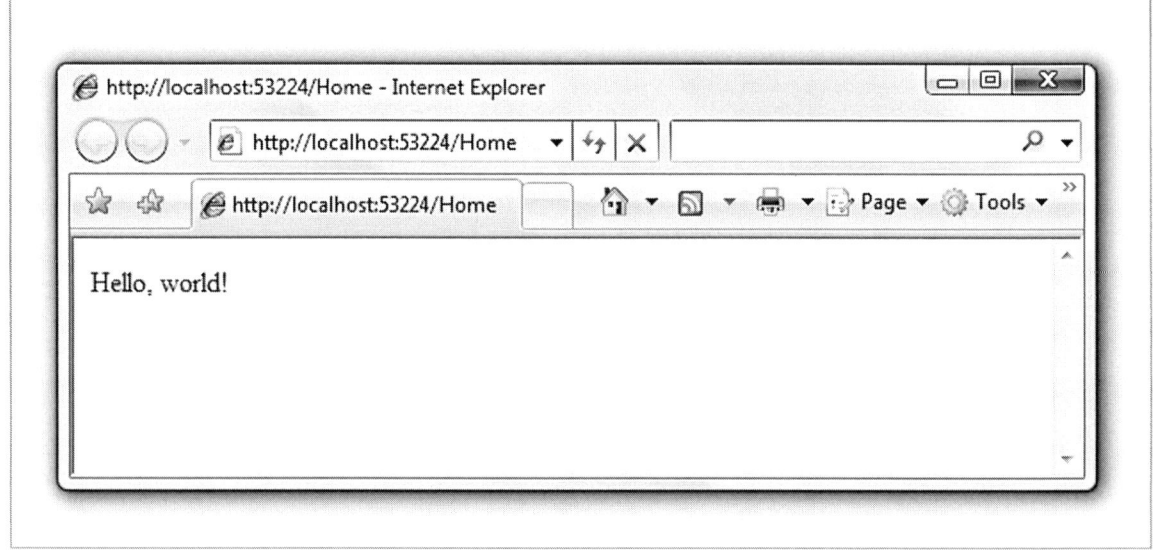

## How Does It Work?

In MVC architecture, *controllers* are responsible for handling incoming requests. In ASP.NET MVC, controllers are just simple C# classes (usually derived from `System.Web.Mvc.Controller`, the framework's built-in controller base class).[7] Each public method on a controller class is an *action method*, which means you can invoke it from the web via some URL. Right now, you have a controller class called `HomeController` and an action method called `Index()`.

---

[7] Actually, you can build ASP.NET MVC applications using any .NET language (e.g., Visual Basic or IronPython). But since C# is the focus of this book, I'll just say "C#" from now on.

There's also a *routing system*, which decides how URLs map onto particular controllers and actions. Under the default configuration, all of the following URLs go to HomeController and its Index() action:

- /
- /Home
- /Home/Index

So, when a browser requests http://*yoursite*/Home, it gets back the output from HomeController's Index() method.

---

**Note**      As of Preview 4, there's a special Default.aspx file added to the root of your ASP.NET MVC project. It's hard-coded to redirect the visitor to /Home. This is a workaround for a bug in Visual Studio's built-in development web server (without a Default.aspx file, the built-in server will not execute the handler for the root URL (i.e., ~/), and will return a directory listing instead). That's not very elegant (do you *always* want the site's main page to appear at ~/Home?), and behaves oddly when deployed to IIS. IIS 6 executes Default.aspx, redirecting the visitor to ~/Home, whereas IIS 7 executes HomeController at ~/, without requiring a redirection. Note that in Visual Studio 2008 SP1, Microsoft fixed the underlying bug in the built-in web server. We've yet to see how ASP.NET MVC will handle this in its final release.

---

# Rendering Web Pages

If you've made it this far, well done—your installation is working perfectly, and you've already created a working, minimal controller. The next step is to produce some HTML output.

# Creating and Rendering a View

Your existing controller, `HomeController`, sends a plain-text `string` to the browser. That's fine for debugging, but in real applications, you're more likely to generate an HTML document, and you'd do so by using a *view template* (also known simply as a *view*).

By convention, views for `HomeController` go into the `/Views/Home` folder. Use Solution Explorer to find `/Views/Home`, right-click it, and choose Add ➤ New Item. From the pop-up that appears, choose MVC View Page (not Web Form!), and call it `Index.aspx` (see Figure 2-6). By following this naming convention, you've associated your new view with the `Index` action method on `HomeController`.

*Figure 2-6. Adding a new MVC View Page*

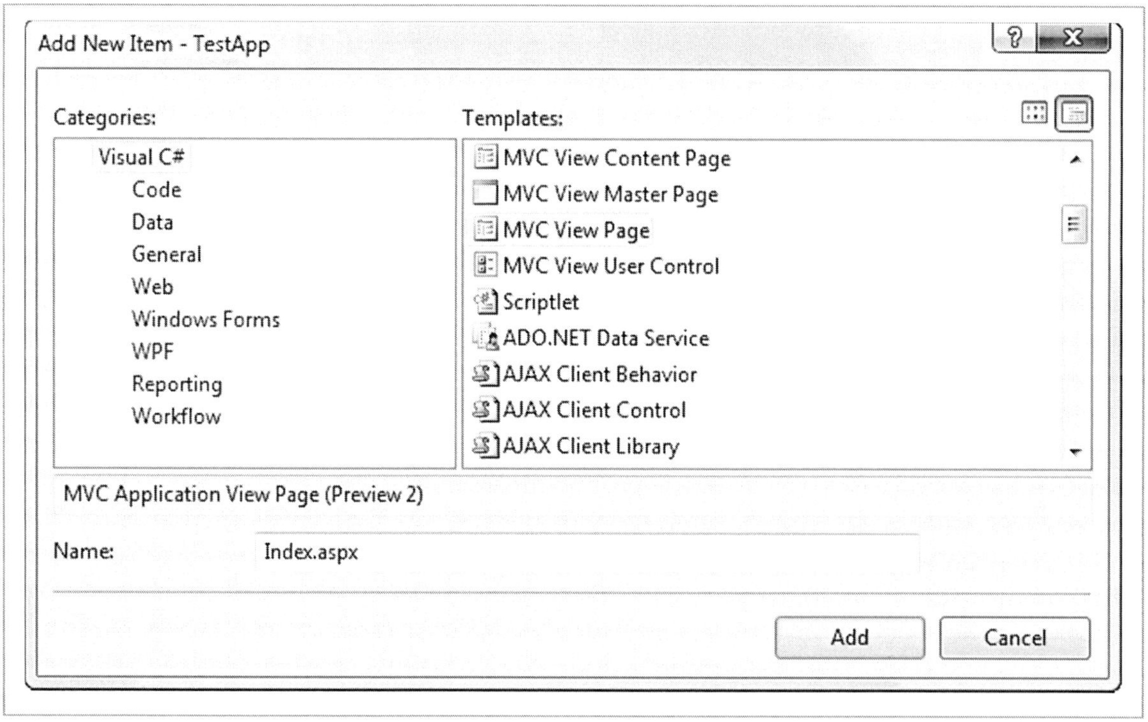

As Visual Studio's HTML markup editor appears,[8] you'll see something familiar: an HTML page template prepopulated with the usual collection of elements (`<html>`, `<body>`, etc.). Let's move the `Hello, world!` greeting into the view. Replace the `<body>` section of the HTML template with the following:

```
<body>
   Hello, world (from the view)!
</body>
```

Then update `HomeController`'s `Index()` action method so that it renders your new view:

```
public class HomeController : Controller
{
    public ViewResult Index()
    {
        return View();
    }
}
```

Press F5 again, and you should see your view template at work, as in Figure 2-7.

---

[8] If instead you get Visual Studio's WYSIWYG designer, switch to Source view by clicking Source (located near the bottom of the screen) or by pressing Shift+F7.

*Figure 2-7. Output from the view*

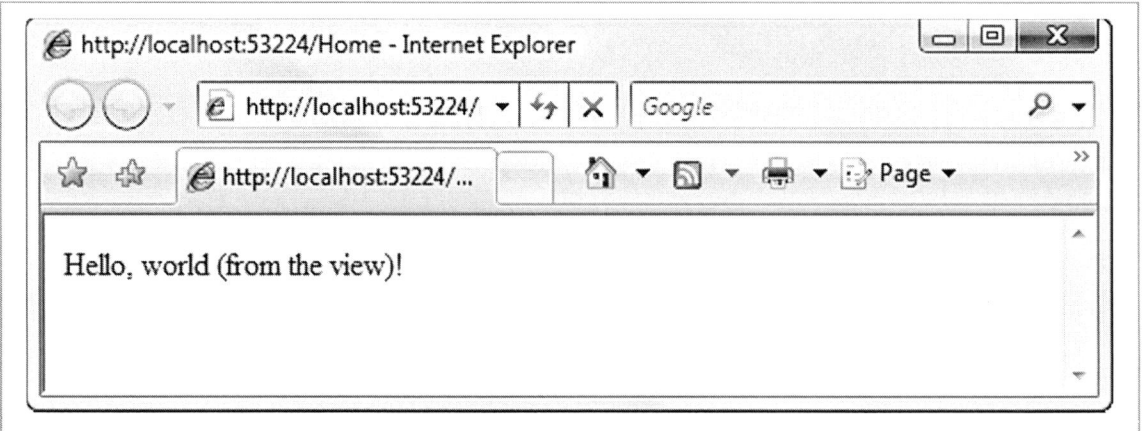

Previously, your `Index()` action method simply returned a `string`, so the MVC Framework had nothing to do but send that `string` as the HTTP response. Now, though, you're returning an object of type `ViewResult`, which instructs the MVC Framework to render a view. You didn't specify a view name, so it picks the conventional one for this action method (i.e., `/Views/Home/Index.aspx`).

There are other types of objects you can return that instruct the framework to do different things. For example, a `RedirectResult` performs a redirection, and an `HttpUnauthorizedResult` forces the visitor to log in. All of these *action results* derive from a common base class called `ActionResult`. The action results system lets you encapsulate and reuse common response types, and it simplifies unit testing tremendously.

## Adding Dynamic Output

Of course, the whole point of a web application platform is the ability to construct and display *dynamic* output. In ASP.NET MVC, it's the controller's job to construct some data, and the view's job to render it as HTML. This separation of concerns keeps your application tidy. The data is passed from controller to view using a data structure called `ViewData`.

As a simple example, alter your HomeController's Index() action method (again) to add a string into ViewData:

```
public ViewResult Index()
{
    int hour = DateTime.Now.Hour;
    ViewData["greeting"] = (hour < 12 ? "Good morning" : "Good afternoon");
    return View();
}
```

And update your Index.aspx view template to display it:

```
<body>
    <%= ViewData["greeting"] %>, world (from the view)!
</body>
```

---

**Note**      Here, we're using *inline code* (the <%= ... %> block). This practice is sometimes frowned upon in the ASP.NET WebForms world, but it's your route to happiness with ASP.NET MVC. Put aside any prejudices you might hold right now—as you learn more about MVC's separation of concerns, you'll see that inline code is a sensible place to put very simple presentation-only logic.

---

Not surprisingly, when you run the application again (press F5), your dynamically chosen greeting will appear in the browser (Figure 2-8).

*Figure 2-8. Dynamically generated output*

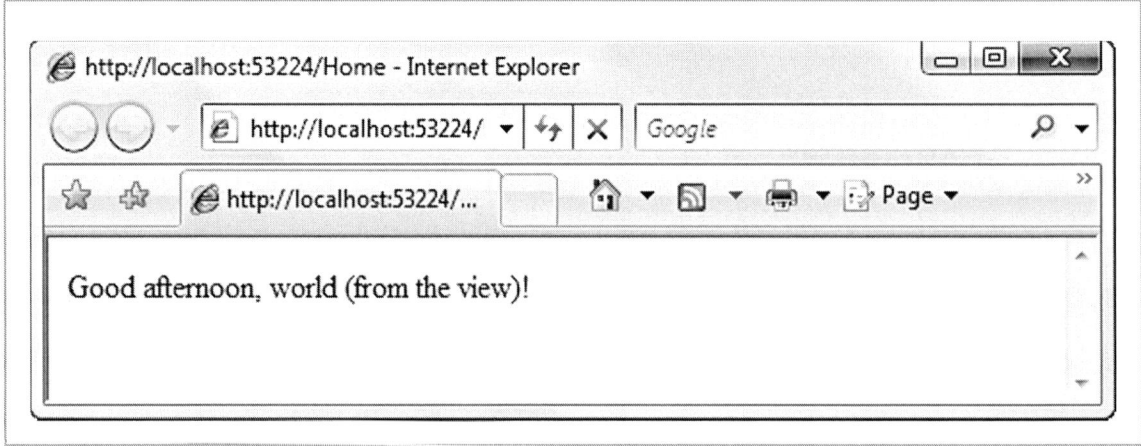

# A Starter Application

In the remainder of this chapter, you'll learn some more of the basic ASP.NET MVC principles by building a simple data entry application. The goal here is just to see the platform in operation, so I'll show you how to create it without slowing down to explain how each bit works behind the scenes.

Don't worry if some parts of MVC architecture seem unfamiliar to you. In the next chapter, you'll find a fuller discussion of its goals and principles.

## The Story

Your friend is having a New Year's party, and she's asked you to create a web site that allows invitees to send back an electronic RSVP. This application, PartyInvites, will

- Have a home page showing information about the party

- Have an RSVP form into which invitees can enter their contact details and say whether or not they will attend

- Validate form submissions, displaying a thank you page if successful

- E-mail details of completed RSVPs to the party organizer

I can't promise that it will be enough for you to retire as a Web 3.0 billionaire, but it's a good start. You can implement the first bullet point feature immediately: just add some HTML to your existing Index.aspx view:

```
<body>
    <h1>New Year's Party</h1>
    <p>
        <%= ViewData["greeting"] %>! We're going to have an exciting party.
        (To do: sell it better. Add pictures or something.)
    </p>
</body>
```

## Linking Between Pages

There's going to be an RSVP form, so you'll need to place a link to it. Update Index.aspx:

```
<body>
    <h1>New Year's Party</h1>
    <p>
        <%= ViewData["greeting"] %>! We're going to have an exciting party.
        (To do: sell it better. Add pictures or something.)
    </p>
    <%= Html.ActionLink("RSVP Now", "ShowRSVPForm") %>
</body>
```

---

**Note**    Html.ActionLink is an *HTML helper method*. The framework comes with a built-in collection of useful HTML helpers that give you a convenient shorthand for rendering not just HTML links, but also text input boxes, check boxes, selection boxes, and even custom controls. When you type <%= Html., you'll see Visual Studio's IntelliSense spring forward to let you pick from the available HTML helper methods.

---

Run the project again, and you'll see the new link (Figure 2-9).

*Figure 2-9. A view with a link*

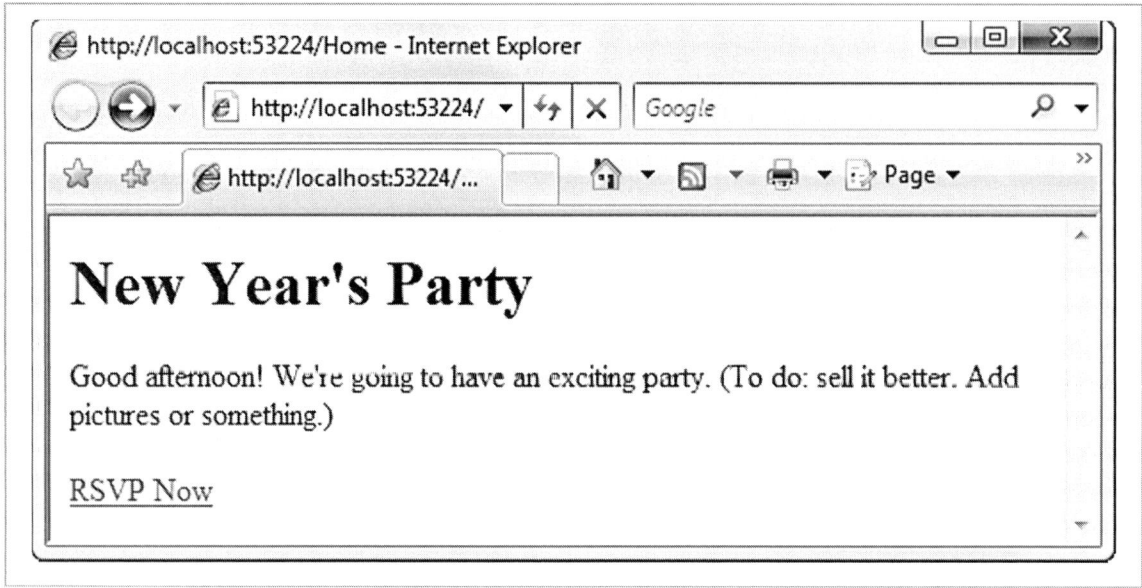

But if you click the RSVP Now link, you'll get a 404 Not Found error. Check out the browser's address bar: it will read
`http://`*`yourserver`*`/Home/ShowRSVPForm`.

That's because `Html.ActionLink()` inspected your routing configuration and figured out that, under the current (default) configuration, that's the URL for an action called `ShowRSVPForm()` on `HomeController`. Unlike in ASP.NET WebForms, PHP, and many other web development platforms, URLs in ASP.NET MVC don't correspond to files on the server's hard disk—instead, they're mapped through a routing configuration onto a controller and action method. Each action method automatically has its own URL; you don't need to create a separate "page" or class for each URL.

Of course, the reason for the 404 Not Found error is that you haven't yet defined any action method called `ShowRSVPForm()`. Add a new method to your `HomeController` class:

```
public ViewResult ShowRSVPForm()
{
    // When you specify a view name explicitly, it doesn't
    // have to match the name of the action method
    return View("RSVPForm");
}
```

If you run the project now and click the RSVP Now link, you'll get the attractive error screen shown in Figure 2-10.

*Figure 2-10. ASP.NET MVC's error screen when it can't find your view*

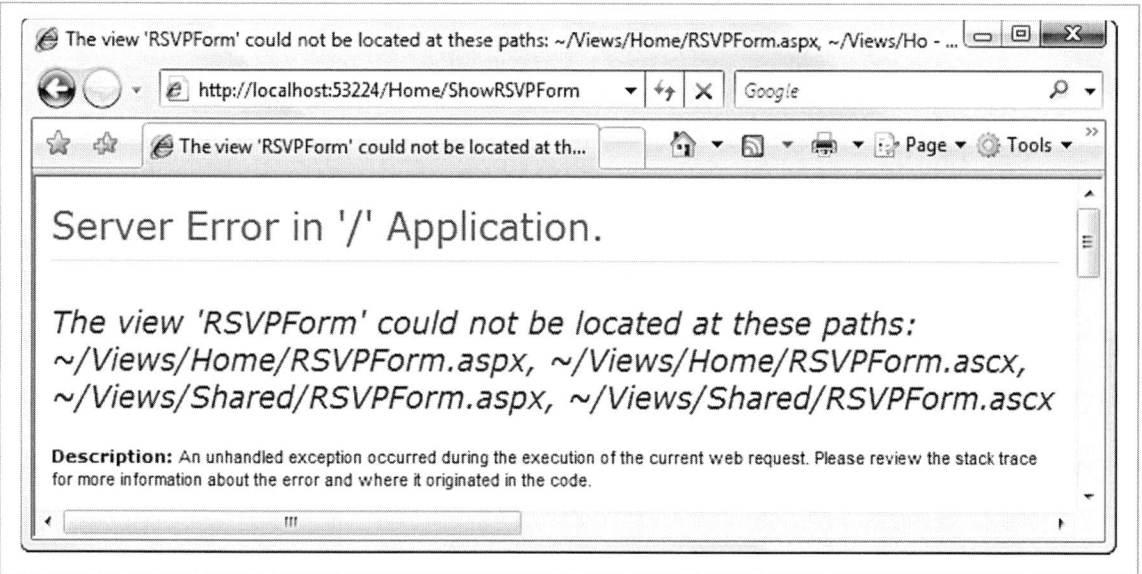

It's more helpful than your average error message, because it clearly shows how the framework looked for the requested view template in each of those four locations in turn, but found nothing, and so gave up. Your next step, of course, is to use Solution Explorer to add a new MVC View Page at the location /Views/Home/RSVPForm.aspx. You can leave its contents blank.

Once you've done that (and recompiled), you can go back and click your RSVP Now link. Instead of the error message, you'll get the blank page.

## Designing a Data Model

You could go right ahead and fill in `RSVPForm.aspx` with HTML form controls, but before you do that, take a step back and think about the application you're building.

In MVC, *M* stands for *model*, and it's the most important character in the story. Your *model* is a software representation of the real-world objects, processes, and rules that make up the subject matter, or *domain*, of your application. A well-crafted MVC application isn't just an ad hoc collection of controllers and views; there's also a model: a recognizable software component in its own right. It's the central keeper of domain logic (i.e., business processes and rules). Everything else (controllers and views) is merely plumbing needed to expose the model's operations and data to the Web. The next chapter will cover this architecture, with comparisons to others, in more detail.

You don't need much of a domain model for the `PartyInvites` application, but there is one obvious type of model object that we'll call `GuestResponse`. This object will be responsible for storing, validating, and ultimately confirming an invitee's RSVP.

### Adding a Model Class

Use Solution Explorer to add a new blank C# class called `GuestResponse.cs` inside the `/Models` folder, and then give it some properties:

```
public class GuestResponse
{
    public string Name { get; set; }
    public string Email { get; set; }
    public string Phone { get; set; }
    public bool? WillAttend { get; set; }
}
```

This class uses C# 3 *automatic properties* (i.e., { get; set; }). (If you haven't caught up with C# 3 yet, you might want to check out the Appendix, which explains C# 3 syntax in detail.)

Also notice that WillAttend is a *nullable* bool (the question mark makes it nullable). This creates a tri-state value: True, False, or null (the latter value for when the guest hasn't yet specified whether they'll attend).

## Building a Strongly Typed Form

It's now time to work on RSVPForm.aspx, turning it into a form for editing instances of GuestResponse. Go back to RSVPForm.aspx, but this time go into its code-behind class (choose View ➤ Code, or press F7).

At the moment, you have a class called RSVPForm that's derived from ViewPage (the framework's default base class for view pages). This is called a *loosely typed* view page, because it can only use dictionary semantics to access data in its ViewData collection (e.g., <%= ViewData["greeting"] %>).

There is another standard base class for view pages, ViewPage<T>, the base class for *strongly typed* view pages. Strongly typed view pages can still use dictionary semantics, plus they have access to a special object, ViewData.Model, of the generic type T. If your view page largely deals with a specific type of model object, you can use that type as the generic parameter T, and then you can access its properties in a strongly typed fashion (e.g., <%= ViewData.Model.Phone %>).

In this example, you're specifically working with a GuestResponse object, so change RSVPForm.aspx's code-behind class to derive from ViewPage<GuestResponse>:

```
public partial class RSVPForm : ViewPage<GuestResponse>
{
}
```

Compile it to make sure it works (Build ➤ Build Solution, or Ctrl+Shift+B). Now, switching back to the ASPX template for `RSVPForm.aspx`, you can use ASP.NET MVC's built-in helper methods to construct an HTML form:

```
<body>
    <h1>RSVP</h1>

    <% using(Html.Form("Home", "SubmitRSVP", FormMethod.Post)) { %>
        <p>Your name: <%= Html.TextBox("Name", ViewData.Model.Name) %></p>
        <p>Your email: <%= Html.TextBox("Email", ViewData.Model.Email)%></p>
        <p>Your phone: <%= Html.TextBox("Phone", ViewData.Model.Phone)%></p>
        <p>
            <%= Html.RadioButton("WillAttend", "Yes, I'll be there!", "True",
                            ViewData.Model.WillAttend == true) %>
            <%= Html.RadioButton("WillAttend", "No, sorry, I can't come.",
                            "False", ViewData.Model.WillAttend == false)%>
        </p>
        <input type="submit" value="Submit RSVP" />
    <% } %>
</body>
```

For each form element, you're specifying a *name* for the rendered HTML tag (e.g., `Email`) and an *initial value* for that form element (e.g., `ViewData.Model.Email`). Because you have a strongly typed view page derived from `ViewPage<GuestResponse>`, you'll get full IntelliSense each time you reference `ViewData.Model` (Figure 2-11).

*Figure 2-11. IntelliSense in a strongly typed view*

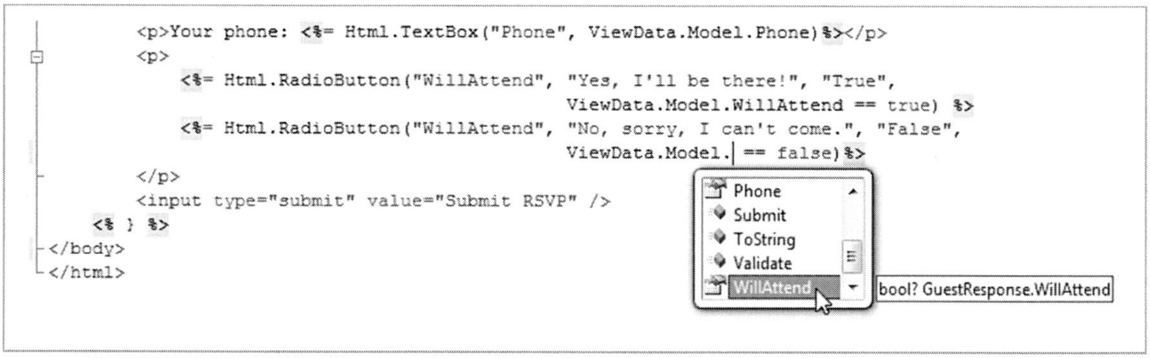

```
          <p>Your phone: <%= Html.TextBox("Phone", ViewData.Model.Phone)%></p>
          <p>
              <%= Html.RadioButton("WillAttend", "Yes, I'll be there!", "True",
                                   ViewData.Model.WillAttend == true) %>
              <%= Html.RadioButton("WillAttend", "No, sorry, I can't come.", "False",
                                   ViewData.Model.| == false)%>
          </p>
          <input type="submit" value="Submit RSVP" />
      <% } %>
  </body>
  </html>
```

| |
|---|
| 🔲 Phone |
| ◆ Submit |
| ◆ ToString |
| ◆ Validate |
| 🔲 **WillAttend**    bool? GuestResponse.WillAttend |

---

**Tip**        In this example, the form element names (e.g., Email) match the property name used for the initial value (e.g., ViewData.Model.Email). So, you could actually use a shorthand syntax and omit the initial value (e.g., just write <%= Html.TextBox("Email") %>). The MVC Framework would pick an initial value by looking for the correspondingly named property on ViewData.Model.

---

Note that these radio button elements mark themselves as selected only when the incoming WillAttend value matches their own value. If WillAttend is null, neither will start selected.

The last thing to point out is the <% using(Html.Form(...)) { ... } %> helper syntax. This creative use of C#'s using syntax puts an opening <form> tag where it first appears, and a closing </form> tag at the end of the using block. This particular one renders a form that POSTs to an as-yet-undefined action called SubmitRSVP() on HomeController, so this will render as follows:

```
<form action="/Home/SubmitRSVP" method="post" >
    ... contents go here ...
</form>
```

**Note** "Traditional" ASP.NET WebForms requires you to surround your entire page in exactly one *server-side form* (i.e., `<form runat="server">`), which is WebForms' container for ViewState data and postback logic. However, ASP.NET MVC doesn't use server-side forms. It just uses plain, straightforward HTML forms (i.e., `<form>`). You can have as many of them as you like in a single view page, and their output is perfectly clean—it doesn't add any extra hidden fields (e.g., __VIEWSTATE), it doesn't mangle your element IDs, and it doesn't automatically inject any extra JavaScript blocks.

I'm sure you're itching to try your new form out, but if you do so right now, you'll get an error message, as in Figure 2-12.

*Figure 2-12. What happens when you fail to supply a ViewData.Model object*

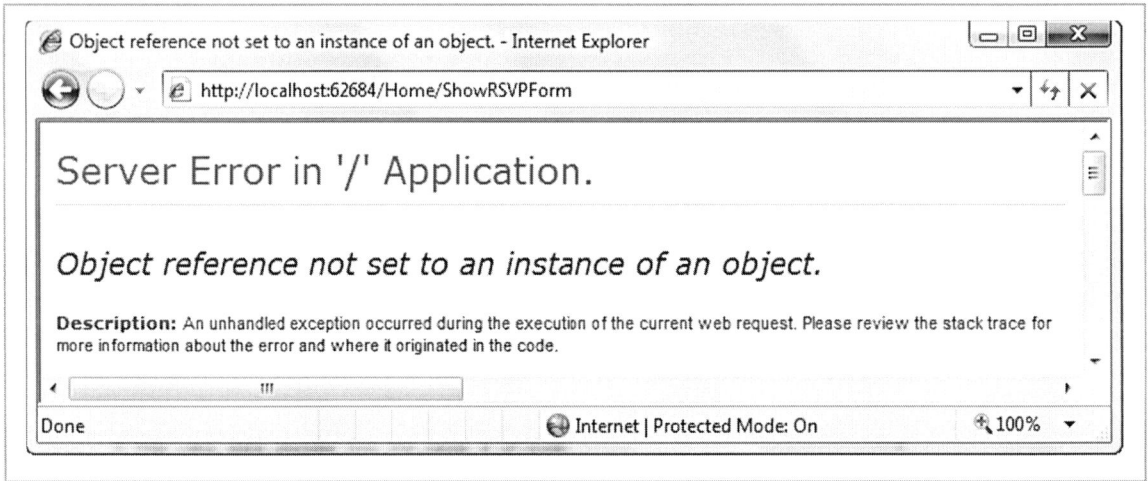

Huh? This is because `RSVPForm.aspx` is now expecting a `ViewData.Model` object of type `GuestResponse`, but `HomeController` isn't passing it one. Solve this by updating `HomeController`'s `ShowRSVP()` action, either like this:

```
public ViewResult ShowRSVPForm()
{
    ViewData.Model = new GuestResponse();
    return View("RSVPForm");
}
```

or equivalently, and more tidily, like this:

```
public ViewResult ShowRSVPForm()
{
    return View("RSVPForm", new GuestResponse());
}
```

Again, you can use Ctrl+dot to import the namespace for `GuestResponse`. Finally, you can see your glorious form in all its raw beauty (Figure 2-13).[9]

---

[9] This book isn't about CSS or web design, so we'll stick with the retro chic "class of 1996" theme. ASP.NET MVC values pure, clean HTML, and gives you total control over your element IDs and layouts, so you'll have no problems using any off-the-shelf web design template or fancy JavaScript effects library.

*Figure 2-13. Output from the RSVPForm.aspx view*

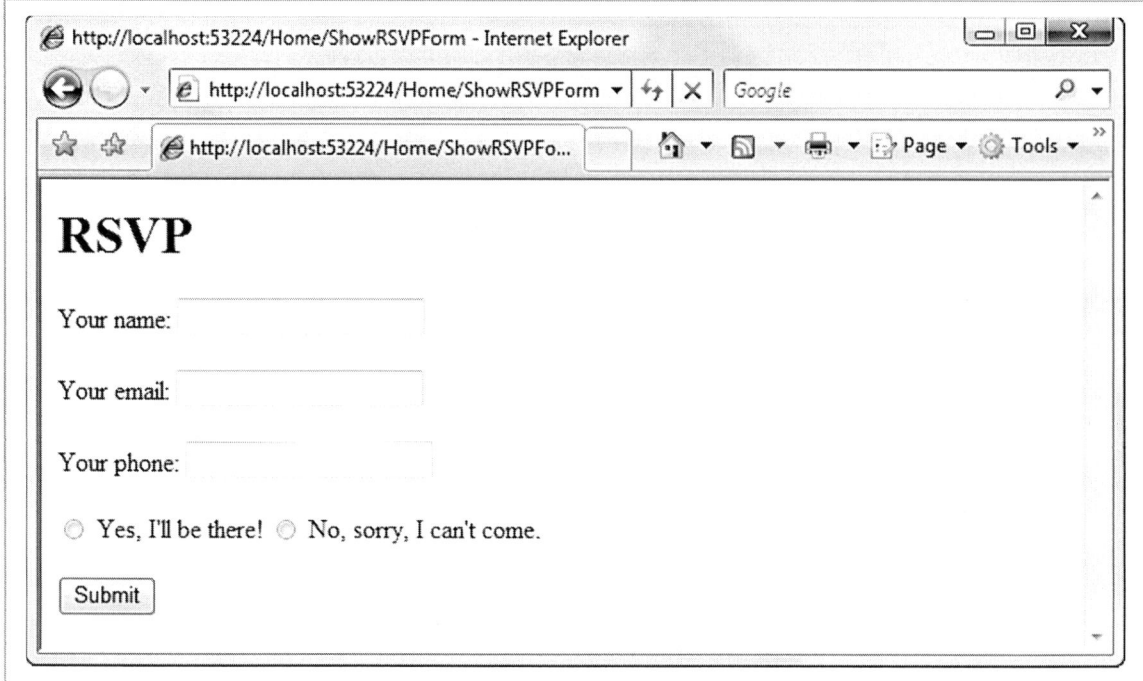

Of course, this form POSTs to an action called SubmitRSVP, which doesn't yet exist, so if you submit the form, you'll get a 404 Not Found error.

## Handling Form Submissions

Create a new action method on HomeController, called SubmitRSVP, along with some code to parse the incoming GuestResponse from the request:

```
public ViewResult SubmitRSVP()
{
    // Construct a GuestResponse object, taking
    // property values from Request.Form
    GuestResponse guestResponse = new GuestResponse();
    BindingHelperExtensions.UpdateFrom(guestResponse, Request.Form);

    // TODO: Email guestResponse to the party organizer
    return View("Thanks", guestResponse);
}
```

Here, `BindingHelperExtensions.UpdateFrom()` inspects the properties exposed by `GuestResponse` and matches them to name/value pairs in the incoming `Request.Form` collection, so you can get a fully populated `GuestResponse` object without having to fetch and assign each property value manually. `UpdateFrom()` will work because you previously named each form element after the property to which it binds (e.g., `<%= Html.TextBox("Email", ViewData.Email) %>`).

To complete the picture, add a new MVC View Page, `/Views/Home/Thanks.aspx`, again derived from `ViewPage<GuestResponse>`, containing the following:

```
<body>
    <h1>Thank you, <%= Html.Encode(ViewData.Model.Name) %>!</h1>
    <% if(ViewData.Model.WillAttend.Value) { %>
        It's great that you're coming.
        The drinks are already in the fridge!
    <% } else { %>
        Sorry to hear you can't make it, but thanks for letting us know.
    <% } %>
</body>
```

You can now fire up your application, fill in the form, submit it, and see a sensible result (Figure 2-14).

---

**Tip**      Protect your application from cross-site scripting (XSS) attacks by HTML-encoding any user input that you echo back. For example, Thanks.aspx contains `<%= Html.Encode(ViewData.Model.Name) %>`, not just `<%= ViewData.Model.Name %>`.

---

*Figure 2-14. Output from the Thanks.aspx view*

## Adding Validation

You may have noticed that so far, there's no validation whatsoever. You can type in any nonsense for an e-mail address, or even just submit a completely blank form.[10] The horror!

It's time to rectify that—but before you go looking for the validation controls, remember that this is an MVC application. Following straightforward software design principles (e.g., separation of concerns), validation is a *model* concern, *not* a UI concern. Validation often reflects business rules, which are most maintainable when expressed coherently in one and only one place, not scattered variously across ASPX and ASCX files. Also, by putting validation right into the model, you ensure that its data integrity is always protected in the same way, no matter what controller or view is connected to it. This is a more robust way of thinking than is encouraged by WebForms-style <asp:XyzValidator> UI controls.

Add a new method, Validate(), to GuestResponse:

---

[10] Which will cause an InvalidOperationException, because Thanks.aspx assumes WillAttend has a non-null value.

```
public class GuestResponse
{
    public string Name { get; set; }
    public string Email { get; set; }
    public string Phone { get; set; }
    public bool? WillAttend { get; set; }

    public string[] Validate()
    {
        var errors = new List<string>();
        if (string.IsNullOrEmpty(Name))
            errors.Add("Name is required");
        if (string.IsNullOrEmpty(Email))
            errors.Add("Email address is required");
        else if (!Regex.IsMatch(Email,
                @"\w[-._\w]*\w@\w[-._\w]*\w\.\w{2,}"))
            errors.Add("That email address is invalid");
        if (string.IsNullOrEmpty(Phone.ToString()))
            errors.Add("Phone number is required");
        if (!WillAttend.HasValue)
            errors.Add("Attendance must be specified");
        return errors.ToArray();
    }
}
```

---

**Note**     As of Preview 4, the MVC Framework doesn't have any built-in validation system. We're expecting some validation facility to appear in the next preview release, and in fact it's pretty much the last big missing piece for the whole MVC Framework. In this chapter, you'll see one way to implement validation manually, but you should expect a tidier alternative (hopefully including client-side validation) to be available when the MVC Framework is finalized.

---

If you're a fan of elegant code, you might want to use a validation framework such as Castle Validator, which lets you collapse all this down to just a few C# attributes attached to properties on the model object (e.g.,

[ValidateEmail]).[11] But for this small application, the preceding technique is simple and readable enough.

---

**Note** You'll need to add using statements for `System.Collections.Generic` and `System.Text.RegularExpressions`. Again, Visual Studio can do this for you with the Ctrl+dot trick.

---

You can now update `SubmitRSVP()` to check for validation errors:

```
public ActionResult SubmitRSVP()
{
    GuestResponse guestResponse - new GuestResponse();
    BindingHelperExtensions.UpdateFrom(guestResponse, Request.Form);

    var errors = guestResponse.Validate();
    if (errors.Count() > 0)
    {
        TempData["errors"] = errors;
        return RedirectToAction("ShowRSVPForm");
    }
    else
    {
        // TODO: Email guestResponse to the party organizer
        return View("Thanks", guestResponse);
    }
}
```

This method now returns a general `ActionResult`, rather than a specific action result subclass (such as `ViewResult`). That's because it *might* return a `ViewResult`, or it *might* return a `RedirectToRouteResult`. The code also introduces two further ASP.NET MVC features:

---

[11] A validation framework could let you use localization to avoid hard-coded validation error messages, too.

- `RedirectToAction()`, which causes an HTTP 302 redirection (i.e., like `Response.Redirect()`) to whatever URL maps to the specified action method.[12]

- The `TempData` collection, which lets you preserve data over an HTTP redirection. It's like the `Session` collection, except that data items are retained for *only one subsequent HTTP request*. In other words, it cleans up after itself. (Here, you're making the **errors** object available to the next request.)

To display the validation errors, add some new code to `RSVPForm.aspx`:

```
<body>
    <h1>RSVP</h1>

    <% if(TempData["errors"] != null) { %>
        <p>Sorry, there was a problem:</p>
        <ul style="color:Red">
            <% foreach(string err in (string[])TempData["errors"]) { %>
                <li><%= err %></li>
            <% } %>
        </ul>
    <% } %>

    (... everything else as before ...)
```

And now, if you try to submit a blank form or enter invalid data, you'll see the validation kick in, as in Figure 2-15.

---

[12] As an alternative to doing a redirection, you could just render the `ShowRSVPForm()` directly. However, you can keep your code simpler if each method has only one main responsibility. That's why I prefer to redirect the visitor back to `ShowRSVPForm()`.

*Figure 2-15. The validation feature working*

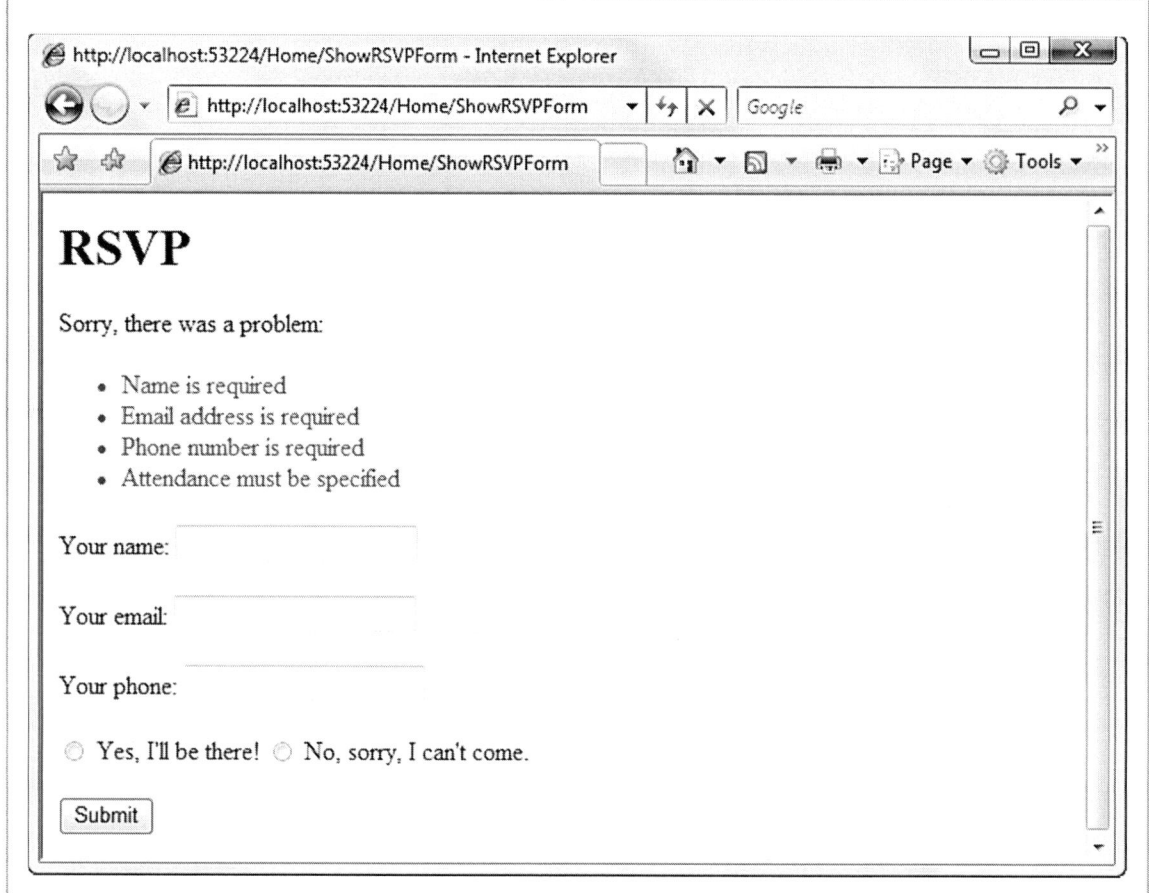

## Preserving Form Data

Right now, there's a bit of a usability problem. When visitors submit an invalid form, they get a nice set of validation messages, but they also lose all the data they entered, forcing them to type it again. This is one of the worst sins of web development. Fortunately, it's very easy to fix. You can simply use `TempData` to preserve the submitted `GuestResponse` object, and assign it back as `ViewData.Model`. First, update `SubmitRSVP()`:

```
if (errors.Count() > 0)
{
    TempData["errors"] = errors;
    TempData["previousData"] = guestResponse;
    return RedirectToAction("ShowRSVPForm");
}
```

Then update `ShowRSVPForm()` to receive the data:

```
public ViewResult ShowRSVPForm()
{
  return View("RSVPForm", TempData["previousData"] ?? new GuestResponse());
}
```

This code uses C#'s double–question mark (??) *null-coalescing* operator. That means it will use `TempData["previousData"]` if available; and if not, it will create a new `GuestResponse()`.

Try it: you'll now get the desired behavior of preserving whatever form data was entered, with validation messages disappearing each time you enter valid data. Finally, when `GuestResponse` considers itself valid, `SubmitRSVP()` displays `Thanks.aspx`.

## Finishing Off

The last requirement is to e-mail completed RSVPs to the party organizer. You could do this directly from an action method, but it's more logical to put this behavior into the model. After all, there could be other UIs that work with this same model and want to submit GuestResponse objects, too. Add another method to GuestResponse:[13]

```
public void Submit()
{
  if (this.Validate().Count() > 0)
    throw new InvalidOperationException("Can't submit while invalid");
  else
  {
    // Send via email
    string text = "";
    string newline = Environment.NewLine;
    text += "Date: " + DateTime.Now.ToString("yyyy-MM-dd hh:mm") + newline;
    text += "RSVP from: " + Name + newline;
    text += "Email: " + Email + newline;
    text += "Phone: " + Phone + newline;
    text += "Can come: " + (WillAttend.Value ? "Yes" : "No");

    SmtpClient smtpClient = new SmtpClient();
    smtpClient.Send(new MailMessage(
      "rsvps@example.com",                                    // From
      "party-organizer@example.com",                          // To
      Name + (WillAttend.Value ? " will attend":"won't attend"), // Subject
      text                                                    // Body
    ));
  }
}
```

---

[13] You'll need to add using System.Net.Mail; as well.

Call this from SubmitRSVP():

```
// etc
else
{
    guestResponse.Submit();
    return View("Thanks", guestResponse);
}
```

## CONFIGURING SMTPCLIENT

This example uses .NET's SmtpClient API to send e-mail. By default, it takes mail server settings from your web.config file. To configure it to send e-mail through a particular SMTP server, add the following to your web.config file:

```
<configuration>
  <system.net>
    <mailSettings>
      <smtp deliveryMethod="Network">
        <network host="smtp.example.com"/>
      </smtp>
    </mailSettings>
  </system.net>
</configuration>
```

During development, you might prefer just to write e-mail to a local directory, so you can see what's happening without having to set up an actual mail server. To do that, use these settings:

```
<configuration>
  <system.net>
    <mailSettings>
      <smtp deliveryMethod="SpecifiedPickupDirectory"
            from="sender@example.com">
        <specifiedPickupDirectory
                pickupDirectoryLocation="c:\email" />
      </smtp>
    </mailSettings>
  </system.net>
</configuration>
```

This will write `.eml` files to the specified folder (here, `c:\email`), which must already exist. If you double-click `.eml` files in Windows Explorer, they'll open in Outlook Express or Windows Mail.

As promised, the `GuestResponse` model object protects its own integrity by refusing to be submitted when invalid. Of course, it's more common to store objects in a database than to send their details by e-mail, in which case you'll normally validate them before letting them go to the database.

## Summary

You've now seen how to build a simple data entry application using ASP.NET MVC, getting a first glimpse of how MVC architecture works. The example so far hasn't shown the power of the MVC Framework (e.g., we skipped over routing, and there's been no sign of automated testing yet). In the next chapter, you'll drill deeper into the architecture of a good, modern MVC web application.

# Chapter 3: Architecture

Before you go too far with ASP.NET MVC development, it's important to make sure you're familiar with the architecture, design patterns, tools, and techniques that underpin its effective use. By the end of this chapter, you'll know about the following:

- MVC architecture
- Domain models and service classes
- Creating loosely coupled systems using an Inversion of Control (IoC) container
- The basics of automated testing

Much of this chapter doesn't specifically focus on ASP.NET MVC technology itself, but rather discusses wider architectural issues and trends that are useful to understand when using the MVC Framework. You might never have encountered these topics before, or you might already be quite comfortable with some combination of them. Feel free to skip ahead if you hit familiar ground. For most readers, this chapter will contain a lot of new material, and even though it's only a brief outline, it will put you in a strong position to use the MVC Framework effectively.

## Understanding Model-View-Controller Architecture

You should understand by now that ASP.NET MVC applications are built with MVC architecture. But what exactly does that mean, and what is the point of it anyway? In high-level terms, it means that your application will be split into (at least) three distinct pieces:

- A *model*, which represents the items, operations, and rules that are meaningful in the subject matter (domain) of your application. In banking, such items might include bank accounts and credit limits, operations might include funds transfers, and rules might require that accounts stay within credit limits. The model also holds the *state* of your application's universe at the present moment, but is totally disconnected from any notion of a UI.

- A set of *views*, which describe how to render some portion of the model as a visible UI, but otherwise contain no logic.

- A set of *controllers*, which handle incoming requests, perform operations on the model, and choose a view to render back to the user.

There are many variations on the MVC pattern, each having its own terminology and slight difference of emphasis, but they all have the same primary goal: *separation of concerns*. By keeping a clear division between concerns, your application will be easier to maintain and extend over its lifetime, no matter how large it becomes. The following discussion will not labor over the precise academic or historical definitions of each possible twist on MVC; instead, you will learn why MVC is important and how it works effectively in ASP.NET MVC.

In some ways, the easiest way to understand MVC is to understand what it is *not*, so let's start by considering the alternatives.

## The Smart UI (Anti-Pattern)

To build a Smart UI application, a developer first constructs a UI, usually by dragging a series of UI widgets onto a canvas,[14] and then fills in event handler code for each possible button click or other UI event. All application logic resides in these event handlers; logic to accept and validate user input, to perform data access and storage, and to provide feedback by updating the UI. The whole application consists of these event handlers. Essentially, this is what tends to come out by default when you put a novice in front of Visual Studio.

---

[14] Or, in ASP.NET WebForms, by writing a series of tags endowed with the special `runat="server"` attribute.

In this design, there's no separation of concerns whatsoever. Everything is fused together, arranged only in terms of the different UI events that may occur. When logic or business rules need to be applied in more than one handler, the code is usually copied and pasted, or certain randomly chosen segments are factored out into static *utility* classes. For so many obvious reasons, this kind of design pattern is often called an *anti-pattern*.

Let's not sneer at Smart UIs for too long. We've all developed applications like this, and in fact, the design has genuine advantages that make it the best possible choice in certain cases:

- It delivers visible results extremely quickly. In just days or even hours you might have something reasonably functional to show to a client or boss.

- If a project is so small (and will always remain so small) that complexity will never be a problem, then the costs of a more sophisticated architecture outweigh their benefits.

- It has the most obvious possible association between GUI elements and code subroutines. This leads to a very simple mental model for developers— there's hardly any cognitive friction—which might be the only viable option for development teams with less skill or experience. In that case, attempting a more sophisticated architecture may just waste time and lead to a worse result than Smart UI.

- Copy-paste code has a natural (though perverse) kind of decoupling built-in. During maintenance, you can change an individual behavior or fix an individual bug without fear that your changes will affect any other parts of the application.

You have probably experienced the disadvantages of this design (anti) pattern firsthand. Such applications become exponentially harder to maintain as each new feature is added: there's no particular structure, so you can't possibly remember what each piece of code does; changes may need to be repeated in several places to avoid inconsistencies; and there's obviously no way to set up unit tests. Within one or two person-years, these applications tend to collapse under their own weight.

It's perfectly OK to make a *deliberate* choice to build a Smart UI application when you feel it's the best trade-off of pros and cons for your project (in which case, use classic WebForms, not ASP.NET MVC, because WebForms has an easier event model), as long as your business recognizes the limited life span of the resulting software.

## Separating Out the Domain Model

Given the limitations of Smart UI architecture, there's a widely accepted improvement that yields huge benefits for an application's stability and maintainability.

By identifying the real-world entities, operations, and rules that exist in the industry or subject matter you're targeting (the *domain*), and by creating a representation of that domain in software (usually an object-oriented representation backed by some kind of persistent storage system, such as a relational database), you're creating a *domain model*. What are the benefits of doing this?

- Firstly, it's a natural place to put business rules and other domain logic, so that no matter what particular UI code performs an operation on the domain (e.g., "open a new bank account"), the same business processes occur.

- Secondly, it gives you an obvious way to store and retrieve the state of your application's universe at the current point in time, without duplicating that persistence code everywhere.

- Thirdly, you can design and structure the domain model's classes and inheritance graph according to the same terminology and language used by experts in your domain, permitting a *ubiquitous language* shared by your programmers and your business experts, improving communication and increasing the chance that you deliver what the customer actually wants (e.g., programmers working on an accounting package may never actually understand what an *accrual* is unless their code uses the same terminology).

In a .NET application, it makes sense to keep a domain model in a separate assembly (i.e., a C# class library project—or several of them), so that you're constantly reminded of the distinction between domain model and application UI. You would have a reference from the UI project to the domain model project, but no reference in the opposite direction, because the domain model shouldn't know or care about the implementation of any UI that relies on it. For example, if you send a badly formed record to the domain model, it should return a data structure of validation errors, but would not attempt to display those errors on the screen in any way (that's the UI's job).

## Model-View Architecture

If the only separation in your application is between UI and domain model,[15] it's called *model-view* architecture (Figure 3-1).

### Figure 3-1. Model-view architecture for the Web

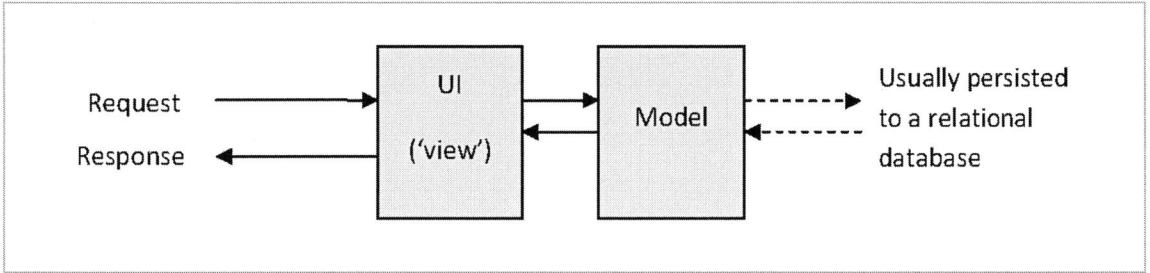

It's far better organized and more maintainable than Smart UI architecture, but still has two striking weaknesses:

- The model component contains a mass of repetitious data access code that's specific to the vendor of the particular database being used. That will be mixed in among code for the business processes and rules of the true domain model, obscuring both.

---

[15] I'm using language that I prefer, but you may substitute the terms *business logic* or *engine* for *domain model*, if you're more familiar with those. I prefer *domain model* because it reminds me to think in terms of domain-driven design (mentioned later).

- Since both model and UI are tightly coupled to their respective database and GUI platforms, it's very hard (if not impossible) to do automated testing on either, or to reuse any of their code with different database or GUI technologies.

## Three-Tier Architecture

Responding in part to these criticisms, *three-tier architecture*[16] cuts persistence code out of the domain model and places that in a separate, third component, called the *data access layer (DAL)*, shown in Figure 3-2.

*Figure 3-2. Three-tier architecture*

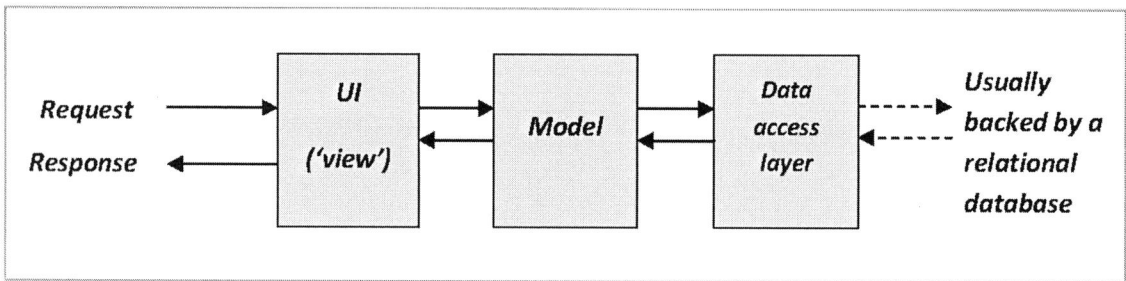

Often—though not necessarily—the DAL is built according to the *repository* pattern, in which an object-oriented representation of a data store acts as a facade on top of a relational database. For example, you might have a class called OrdersRepository, having methods such as GetAllOrders() or DeleteOrder(int orderID). These will use the underlying database to fetch instances of model objects that match stated criteria (or delete them, update them, etc.). If you add in the *abstract factory* pattern, meaning that the model isn't coupled to any concrete implementation of a data repository, but instead accesses repositories only though .NET interfaces or abstract base classes, then the model becomes totally

---

[16] Some argue that it should be called three-*layer* architecture, because the word *tiers* usually refers to physically separate software services (i.e., running on different servers or at least in different OS processes). That distinction doesn't matter for this discussion, however.

decoupled from the database technology. That means you can easily set up automated tests for its logic, using fake or mock repositories to simulate different conditions. You'll hear more about this technique later in the chapter.

Three-tier is among the most widely adopted architectures for business software today, because it can provide a good separation of concerns without being too complicated, and because it places no constraints over how the UI is implemented, so it's perfectly compatible with a *forms-and-controls*–style GUI platform such as Windows Forms or ASP.NET WebForms.

Three-tier architecture is perfectly good for describing the overall design of a software product, but it doesn't address what happens *inside* the UI layer. That's not very helpful when, as in many projects, the UI component tends to balloon to a vast size, amassing logic like a great rolling snowball. It shouldn't happen, but it does, because it's quicker and easier to attach behaviors directly to an event handler (a la Smart UI) than it is to refactor the domain model. When the UI layer is directly coupled to your GUI platform (Windows Forms, WebForms), it's almost impossible to set up any automated tests on it, so all that sneaky new code escapes any kind of rigor. Three-tier's failure to enforce discipline in the UI layer means, in the worst case, that you can end up with a Smart UI application with a feeble parody of a domain model stuck on its side.

## Model-View-Controller Architecture

Recognizing that even after you've factored out a domain model, UI code can still be big and complicated, MVC architecture splits that UI component in two (Figure 3-3).

## Figure 3-3. MVC architecture for the Web

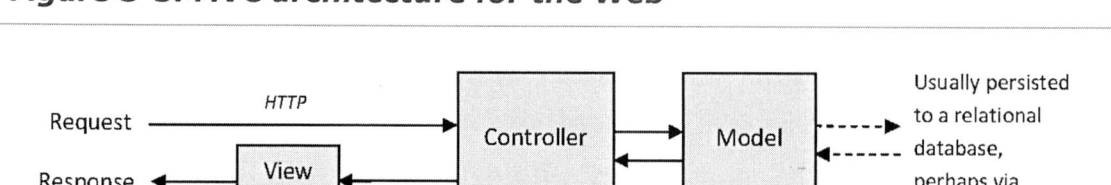

In this architecture, requests are routed to a *controller* class, which processes user input and works with the domain model to handle the request. While the domain model holds domain logic (i.e., business objects and rules), controllers hold application logic, such as navigation through a multistep process or technical details like authentication. When it's time to produce a visible UI for the user, the controller prepares the data to be displayed (the *presentation model*, or `ViewData` in ASP.NET MVC, which for example might be a list of `Product` objects matching the requested category), selects a view, and leaves it to complete the job. Since controller classes aren't coupled to the UI technology (HTML), they are just pure, testable application logic.

Views are simple templates for converting `ViewData` into a finished piece of HTML. They are allowed to contain basic, presentation-only logic, such as the ability to iterate over a list of objects to produce an HTML table row for each object, or the ability to hide or show a section of the page according to a flag in `ViewData`, but nothing more complicated than that. Generally, you're not advised to try automated testing for views' output (the only way would be to test for specific HTML patterns, which is fragile), so you must keep them as simple as possible.

Don't worry if this seems obscure at the moment; you'll get used to it as you use ASP.NET MVC. If you're struggling to understand how a view could be distinct from a controller, as I did when I first tried to learn MVC architecture (does a `TextBox` go into a view or into a controller?), that's probably because you've only used technologies that make the division very hard or impossible, such as Windows Forms or classic ASP.NET WebForms. The answer to the TextBox conundrum is that you'll no longer think in terms of UI widgets, but in terms of requests and responses, which is more appropriate for a web application.

## Implementation in ASP.NET MVC

In ASP.NET MVC, controllers are .NET classes, usually derived from the built-in Controller base class. Each public method on a Controller-derived class is called an *action method*, which is automatically associated with a URL on your configurable URL schema, and after performing some operations, is able to render its choice of view. The mechanisms for both input (receiving data from an HTTP request) and output (rendering a view, redirecting to a different action, etc.) are designed for testability, so during implementation and testing, you're not coupled to any live web server.

The framework supports a choice of view engines, but by default, views are streamlined ASP.NET WebForms pages, usually implemented purely as ASPX templates (with no significant code-behind logic) and always free of ViewState/postback complications. ASPX templates give a familiar, Visual Studio–assisted way to define HTML markup with inline C# code for injecting and responding to ViewData as supplied by the controller.

ASP.NET MVC leaves your model implementation entirely up to you; it provides no particular infrastructure for a domain model, because that's perfectly well handled by a plain vanilla C# class library, .NET's extensive facilities, and your choice of database and data access code or ORM tool. Even though default, newborn ASP.NET MVC projects contain a folder called /Models, it's cleaner to keep your domain model code in a separate Visual Studio class library project. You'll learn more about how to implement a domain model later in this chapter.

## History and Benefits

The term *model-view-controller* has been in use since the late 1970s and the Smalltalk project at Xerox PARC. It was originally conceived as a way to organize some of the first GUI applications, although some aspects of its meaning today, especially in the context of web applications, are a little different than in the original Smalltalk world of "screens" and "tools." For example, the original Smalltalk design expected a view to update itself whenever the underlying data model changed, following the observer synchronization pattern, but that's nonsense when the view is already rendered as a page of HTML in somebody's browser.

These days, the essence of the MVC design pattern turns out to work wonderfully for web applications, because

- Interaction with an MVC application follows a natural cycle of user actions and view updates, with the view assumed to be stateless, which maps well to a cycle of HTTP requests and responses.

- MVC applications enforce a natural separation of concerns. Firstly, that makes code easier to read and understand, and secondly, controller logic is decoupled from the mess of HTML, so the bulk of the application's UI layer can be subject to automated tests.

ASP.NET MVC is hardly the first web platform to adopt MVC architecture. Ruby on Rails is a recent MVC poster child, but Apache Struts, Spring MVC, and many others have already proven its benefits.

# Variations on Model-View-Controller

You've seen the core design of an MVC application, especially as it's commonly used in ASP.NET MVC, but others interpret MVC differently, adding, removing, or changing components according to the scope and subject of their project.

## Where's the Data Access Code?

MVC architecture places no constraints on how the model component is implemented. You can choose to perform data access through abstract repositories if you wish, but it's still MVC even if you don't.

## Putting Domain Logic Directly into Controllers

From looking at the earlier diagram, you might realize that there aren't any strict rules to force developers to correctly split logic between controllers and the domain model. It is certainly possible to put domain logic into a controller, even though you shouldn't, just because it seems expedient at some pressured moment. The best way to protect against the indiscipline of merging model and controllers accidentally is to require good automated test coverage, because even from the naming of such tests it will be obvious when logic has been sited inappropriately.

To save time, most ASP.NET MVC demonstrations and sample code abandon the distinction between controllers and the domain model altogether, in what you might call "controller-view" architecture. This is inadvisable for a real application because it loses the benefits of a domain model, as listed earlier. You'll learn more about domain modeling in the next part of this chapter.

## Model-View-Presenter

Model-view-presenter (MVP) is a recent variation on MVC that's designed to fit more easily with stateful GUI platforms such as Windows Forms or ASP.NET WebForms. You don't need to know about MVP when you're using ASP.NET MVC, but it's worth explaining what it is so you can avoid confusion.

In this twist, the *presenter* has the same responsibilities as MVC's controller, plus it also takes a more hands-on relationship to the stateful view, directly editing the values displayed in its UI widgets according to user input (instead of letting the view render itself from a template). There are two main flavors:

- *Passive view*, in which the view contains no logic, and merely has its UI widgets manipulated by the presenter

- *Supervising controller*, in which the view may be responsible for certain presentation logic, such as data binding, having been given a reference to some data source in the model

The difference between the two flavors is quite subjective and simply relates to how intelligent the view is allowed to be. Either way, the presenter is decoupled from the GUI technology, so its logic can be followed easily and is suitable for automated testing.

Some folks contend that ASP.NET WebForms' code-behind model is like an MVP design (supervising controller), in which the ASPX markup is the view and the code-behind class is the presenter. However, in reality, ASPX pages and their code-behind classes are so tightly fused that you can't slide a hair between them. Consider, for example, a grid's `ItemDataBound` event—that's a view concern, but here it's handled in the code-behind class: it doesn't do justice to MVP. There are ways to implement a genuine MVP design with WebForms by accessing the control hierarchy only through a C# interface type, but it's complicated and you're forever fighting against the platform. Many have tried, and many have given up.

ASP.NET MVC follows the MVC pattern rather than MVP because MVC remains more popular and is arguably simpler for a web application.

## Domain Modeling

You've already seen how it makes sense to take the real-world objects, processes, and rules from your software's subject matter and encapsulate them in a component called a *domain model*. This component is the heart of your software; it's your software's universe. Everything else (including controllers and views) is just a technical detail designed to support or permit interaction with the domain model. Eric Evans, a leader in domain-driven design (DDD), puts it well:

> *The part of the software that specifically solves problems from the domain model usually constitutes only a small portion of the entire software system, although its importance is disproportionate to its size. To apply our best thinking, we need to be able to look at the elements of the model and see them as a system. We must not be forced to pick them out of a much larger mix of objects, like trying to identify constellations in the night sky. We need to decouple the domain objects from other functions of the system, so we can avoid confusing domain concepts with concepts related only to software technology or losing sight of the domain altogether in the mass of the system.*

*Domain Driven Design: Tackling Complexity in the Heart of Software*, by Eric Evans, Addison-Wesley (2004)

ASP.NET MVC contains no specific technology related to domain modeling (instead relying on what it inherits from the .NET Framework and ecosystem), so this book has no chapter on domain modeling. Nonetheless, modeling is the *M* in MVC, so I cannot ignore the subject altogether. For the next portion of this chapter, you'll see a quick example of implementing a domain model with .NET and SQL Server, using a few of the core techniques from DDD.

# An Example Domain Model

No doubt you've already experienced the process of brainstorming a domain model in your previous projects. Typically, it involves one or more developers, one or more business experts, a whiteboard, and a lot of cookies. After a while, you'll pull together a first-draft model of the business processes you're going to automate. For example, if you were going to implement an online auctions site, you might get started with something like that shown in Figure 3-4.

*Figure 3-4. First-draft domain model for an auctions system*

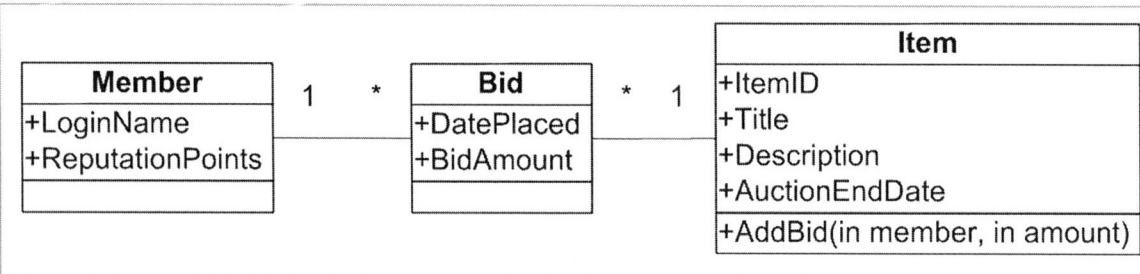

This diagram indicates that the model contains a set of *members* who each hold a set of *bids*, and each bid is for an *item*. An item can have multiple bids from different members.

# Entities and Value Objects

In this example, members and items are *entities*, whereas bids can be expressed as mere *value objects*. In case you're unfamiliar with these domain modeling terms, entities have an ongoing identity throughout their lifetimes, no matter how their attributes vary, whereas value objects are defined purely by the values of their attributes. Value objects are logically immutable, because any change of attribute value would result in a different object. Entities usually have a single unique key (a primary key), whereas value objects need no such thing.

## Ubiquitous Language

A key benefit of implementing your domain model as a distinct component is the ability to design it according to any language and terminology of your choice. Strive to find and stick to a terminology for its entities, operations, and relationships that makes sense not just to developers, but also to your business (domain) experts. Perhaps you might have chosen the terms *users* and *roles*, but in fact your domain experts say *agents* and *clearances*. Even when you're modeling concepts that domain experts don't already have words for, come to an agreement about a shared language—otherwise you can't really be sure that you're faithfully modeling the processes and relationships that the domain expert has in mind. Use this shared language in all communication about the software, whoever you're talking to: it's your *ubiquitous language*.

By getting this ubiquitous language right into your code—into the names of your objects and methods—you're embedding real understanding of your domain into the DNA of your software. Developers will always talk to one another in the language of the code (the names of its objects, database tables, etc.), so try not to allow this to diverge from terms and relationships understandable to business experts, or from the language used in the UI. Otherwise, current and future developers are more likely to misinterpret new feature requests or bug reports, or will confuse users by saying "The user has no access role for that node" (which sounds like the software is broken), instead of "The agent doesn't have clearance on that file."

Don't overgeneralize your domain model. We programmers have a tendency to want to model not just one particular business reality, but every possible reality (e.g., in the auctions example, by replacing "members" and "items" with a general notion of "resources" linked not by "bids" but by "relationships"). By failing to constrain a domain model along the same lines that a particular business in a particular industry operates, you are rejecting any real insight into its workings, and will struggle in the future to implement features that will seem to you like awkward special cases in your elegant metaworld. Constraints are not limitations; they are insight.

Be ready to refactor your domain model as often as is necessary. DDD experts say that any change to the ubiquitous language is a change to the software. If you let the software model drift out of sync with your current understanding of the business domain, performing awkward translations in the UI layer to present up-to-date concepts despite the underlying impedance mismatch, your model component will become a real drain on developer effort. Aside from being a bug magnet, this could mean that some apparently simple feature requests turn out to be incredibly hard to implement, and you won't be able to explain it to your clients.

## Aggregates and Simplification

Take another look at the auctions example diagram (Figure 3-4). As it stands, it doesn't offer much guidance when it comes to implementation with C# and SQL Server. If you load a member into memory, should you also load all their bids, and all the items associated with those bids, and all the other bids for those items, and all the members who have placed all those other bids? When you delete something, how far does that deletion cascade through the object graph? If you want to impose validation rules that involve relationships across objects, where do you put those rules? And this is just a trivial example—how much more complicated will it get in real life?

The classic way to break down this complexity is to arrange domain entities into groups called *aggregates*. Figure 3-5 shows how you might do it in the auctions example.

## Figure 3-5. Auctions domain model with aggregates

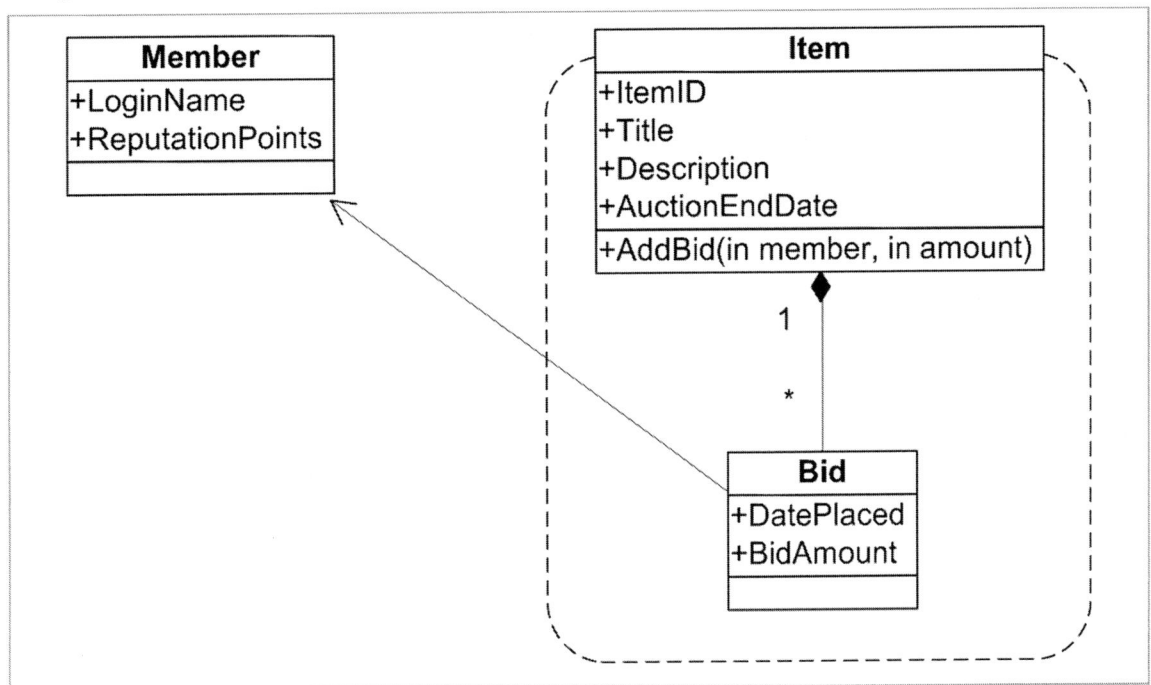

Each aggregate has a *root* entity, which defines the identity of the whole aggregate, and acts as the "boss" of the aggregate for the purposes of validation and persistence. The aggregate is a single unit when it comes to data changes, so choose aggregates that relate logically to real business processes—that is, the sets of objects that tend to change as a group (thereby embedding further insight into your domain model).

Objects outside a particular aggregate may only hold persistent references to the root entity, not to any other object inside that aggregate (in fact, ID values for nonroot entities don't even have to be unique outside the scope of their aggregate). This rule reinforces aggregates as atomic units, and ensures that changes inside an aggregate don't cause data corruption elsewhere.

In this example, members and items are both aggregate roots, because they have to be independently accessible, whereas bids are only interesting within the context of an item. Bids are allowed to hold a reference to members, but members can't directly reference bids because that would violate the items aggregate boundary. Keeping relationships one-directional, as much as possible, leads to considerable simplification of your domain model and may well reflect additional insight into the domain. This might be unfamiliar if you've previously thought of a SQL database schema as being your domain model (given that all relationships in a SQL database are bidirectional), but C# can model a wider range of concepts.

A C# representation of our domain model so far looks like this:

```csharp
public class Member
{
    public string LoginName { get; set; } // The unique key
    public int ReputationPoints { get; set; }
}

public class Item
{
    public int ItemID { get; private set; } // The unique key
    public string Title { get; set; }
    public string Description { get; set; }
    public DateTime AuctionEndDate { get; set; }
    public IList<Bid> Bids { get; private set; }
}

public class Bid
{
    public Member Member { get; private set; }
    public DateTime DatePlaced { get; private set; }
    public decimal BidAmount { get; private set; }
}
```

Notice that Bid is immutable (that's as close as you'll get to a true value object[17]) and the other classes' properties are appropriately protected.

---

[17] You can override the equals operator so that two instances are equal when their attributes are equal, if you like, but it's unnecessary for this example.

These classes respect aggregate boundaries in that no references violate the boundary rule.

---

**Note**    In a sense, a C# `struct` (as opposed to a `class`) is immutable, because each assignment creates a new instance, so mutations don't affect other instances. However, for a domain value object, that's not always the type of immutability you're looking for: you often want to prevent *any* changes from happening to *any* instance (after the point of creation), which means all the fields must be read-only. A `class` is just as good as a `struct` for that, and `classes` have many other advantages (e.g., they support inheritance).

---

### Is It Worth Defining Aggregates?

Aggregates bring superstructure into a complex domain model, adding a whole extra level of manageability. They make it easier to define and enforce data integrity rules (an aggregate root can validate the state of the entire aggregate). They give you a natural unit for persistence, so you can easily decide how much of an object graph to bring into memory (perhaps using lazy-loading for references to other aggregate roots). They're the natural unit for cascade deletion, too. And since data changes are atomic within an aggregate, they're an obvious unit for transactions.

On the other hand, they impose restrictions that can sometimes seem artificial—because they *are* artificial—and compromise is painful.

They're not a native concept in SQL Server, nor in most ORM tools, so to implement them well, your team will need discipline and effective communication.

## Keeping Data Access Code in Repositories

Sooner or later, you'll have to think about getting your domain objects into and out of some kind of persistent storage—usually a relational database.

Of course, this concern is purely a matter of today's software technology, not part of the business domain you're modeling. Persistence is an independent concern (real architects say *orthogonal concern*—it sounds much cleverer), so you don't want to mix persistence code with domain model code, either by embedding database access code directly into domain entity methods, or by putting loading or querying code into static methods on those same classes.

The usual way to keep this separation clean is to define *repositories*. These are nothing more than object-oriented representations of your underlying relational database store (or file-based store, or data accessed over a web service, or whatever), acting as a facade over the real implementation. When you're working with aggregates, it's normal to define a separate repository for each aggregate, because aggregates are the natural unit for persistence logic. For example, continuing the auctions example, you might start with the following two repositories (note that there's no need for a BidsRepository, because bids need only be found by following references from item instances):

```
public class MembersRepository
{
    public void AddMember(Member member) { /* Implement me */ }
    public Member FetchByLoginName(string loginName) { /* Implement me */ }
    public void SubmitChanges() { /* Implement me */ }
}

public class ItemsRepository
{
    public void AddItem(Item item) { /* Implement me */ }
    public Item FetchByID(int itemID) { /* Implement me */ }
    public IList<Item> ListItems(int pageSize,int pageIndex)
        { /* Implement me */ }
    public void SubmitChanges() { /* Implement me */ }
}
```

Notice that repositories are concerned *only* with loading and saving data, and contain as little domain logic as is possible. At this point, you can fill in the code for each repository method using whatever data access strategy you prefer. You might call stored procedures, but in this example you'll see how to use an ORM tool (LINQ to SQL) to make your job easier.

You're relying on these repositories being able to figure out what changes they need to save when you call `SubmitChanges()` (by spotting what you've done to its previously returned entities—LINQ to SQL and NHibernate both handle this easily), but you could instead pass specific updated entity instances to, say, a `SaveMember(Member member)` method if that seems easier for your preferred data access technique.

Finally, you can get a whole slew of extra benefits from your repositories by defining them abstractly (e.g., as a .NET interface) and accessing them through the abstract factory pattern, or with an IoC container. That makes it easy to test code that depends on persistence: you can supply a fake or mock repository implementation that simulates any domain model state you like. Also, you can easily swap out the repository implementation for a different one if you later choose to use a different database or ORM tool. You'll see IoC at work with repositories later in this chapter.

## Using LINQ to SQL

Microsoft introduced LINQ to SQL in 2007 as part of .NET 3.5. It's designed to give you a strongly typed .NET view of your database schema and data, dramatically reducing the amount of code you need to write in common data access scenarios, and freeing you from the burden of creating and maintaining stored procedures for every type of query you need to perform. It is an object-relational mapping tool, not yet as mature and sophisticated as alternatives such as NHibernate, but sometimes easier to use, considering its full support for LINQ and its more thorough documentation.

Most demonstrations of LINQ to SQL use it like a quick prototyping tool. You can start with an existing database schema, using a Visual Studio editor to drag tables and stored procedures onto a canvas, and the tool will generate corresponding entity classes and methods automatically. You can then use LINQ queries inside your C# code to retrieve instances of those entities from a *data context* (it converts LINQ queries into SQL at runtime), modify them in C#, and then call SubmitChanges() to write those changes back to the database.

## WHAT'S A DATACONTEXT?

DataContext is your entry point to the whole LINQ to SQL API. It knows how to load, save, and query for any .NET type that has LINQ to SQL mappings (which you can add manually, or by using the visual designer). After it loads an object from the database, it keeps track of any changes you make to that object's properties, so it can write those changes back to the database when you call its SubmitChanges() method. It's lightweight (i.e., inexpensive to construct); it can manage its own database connectivity, opening and closing connections as needed; and it doesn't even require you to remember to close or dispose of it.

While this is excellent in a Smart UI application, there are limitations in multitier architectures, and if you start from a database schema rather than a C# domain model, you've already abandoned a clean domain model design.

There are many different ways to use LINQ to SQL, some of which are described below:

Schema-first with code generation

> *Workflow*: As described previously, use the graphical designer to drag tables and stored procedures onto a canvas, letting it generate classes and data context objects from the existing database schema.

> *Advantages*: This is convenient if you like designing schemas in SQL Server Management Studio. It doesn't require you to create any mapping configuration.

*Disadvantages*: You end up with a poorly encapsulated domain model that exposes persistence concerns everywhere (e.g., by default, all database IDs are exposed and all relationships are bidirectional).

There's currently no support for updating a database schema, other than by wiping out your LINQ to SQL classes and starting over, losing any changes you've made to field accessibility or directions of relationships.

## Code-first with schema generation

*Workflow*: Create a clean, object-oriented domain model and define interfaces for its repositories (at which point you can write unit tests). Now configure LINQ to SQL mappings, either by adding special attributes to your domain classes or by writing an XML configuration file. Generate the corresponding database schema by calling `yourDataContext.CreateDatabase()`. Implement concrete repositories by writing queries against a `DataContext` object.

*Advantages*: You get a clean, object-oriented domain model with proper separation of concerns.

*Disadvantages*: You have to create mappings manually.

There's no built in method for updating your database schema as you go on. After each schema change, you need to drop the database and generate a new one, losing its data (alternatively, you can use a third-party database schema comparison/synchronization tool).

Not all aspects of a SQL database can be generated this way (e.g., triggers).

## Code-first with manual schema creation

*Workflow*: Follow the "code-first with schema generation" design, except don't call `yourDataContext.CreateDatabase()`. Create the corresponding database schema manually instead.

*Advantages*: You get a clean, object-oriented domain model with proper separation of concerns.

It's obvious how to update your database schema as you go on.

*Disadvantages*: You have to create mappings manually.

You have to keep mappings and database schema synchronized manually.

Two domain models

*Workflow*: Create a clean, object-oriented domain model and also a corresponding database schema. Drag the database tables into LINQ to SQL's graphical designer, generating a second, independent set of domain entity classes in a different namespace, and mark them all as `internal`. In your repository implementations, query the LINQ to SQL entities, and then manually convert the results into instances from your clean domain model.

*Advantages*: You get a clean, object-oriented domain model with proper separation of concerns.

You don't have to use LINQ to SQL's mapping attributes or XML configuration.

*Disadvantages*: You have to write extra code to convert between the two domain models.

You can't use LINQ to SQL's change-tracking feature: for any changes in the clean domain model, you have to replay them in the LINQ to SQL domain model manually.

As with method 1, with any changes in your database schema, you will lose any custom settings in the LINQ to SQL configuration.

Considering the pros and cons, my preference (in a nontrivial application) is method 3 (code-first with manual schema creation). It's not very automated, but it's not too much work when you get going. Next, you'll see how to build the auctions example domain model and repositories in this way.

### Implementing the Auctions Domain Model

With LINQ to SQL, you can set up mappings between C# classes and an implied database schema either by decorating the classes with special attributes or by writing an XML configuration file. The XML option has the advantage that persistence artifacts are totally removed from your domain classes, but the disadvantage that it's not so obvious at first glance. For simplicity, I'll compromise here and use attributes.

Here are the auctions domain model classes now fully marked up for LINQ to SQL:[18]

```
using System;
using System.Collections.Generic;
using System.Linq;
using System.Data.Linq.Mapping;
using System.Data.Linq;

[Table(Name="Members")] public class Member
{
    [Column(IsPrimaryKey=true, IsDbGenerated=true,
    AutoSync=AutoSync.OnInsert)]
    internal int MemberID { get; set; }

    [Column] public string LoginName { get; set; }
    [Column] public int ReputationPoints { get; set; }
}

[Table(Name = "Items")] public class Item
{
    [Column(IsPrimaryKey=true, IsDbGenerated=true,
     AutoSync=AutoSync.OnInsert)]
    public int ItemID { get; internal set; }

    [Column] public string Title { get; set; }
    [Column] public string Description { get; set; }
    [Column] public DateTime AuctionEndDate { get; set; }

    [Association(OtherKey = "ItemID")]
    private EntitySet<Bid> _bids = new EntitySet<Bid>();
    public IList<Bid> Bids { get { return _bids.ToList().AsReadOnly(); } }
}
```

---

[18] For this to compile, your project needs a reference to System.Data.Linq.dll.

```
[Table(Name = "Bids")] public class Bid
{
    [Column(IsPrimaryKey=true, IsDbGenerated=true,
     AutoSync=AutoSync.OnInsert)]
    internal int BidID { get; set; }
    [Column] internal int ItemID { get; set; }
    [Column] public DateTime DatePlaced { get; internal set; }
    [Column] public decimal BidAmount { get; internal set; }
    [Column] internal int MemberID { get; set; }

    internal EntityRef<Member> _member;
    [Association(ThisKey = "MemberID", Storage = "_member")]
    public Member Member {
        get { return _member.Entity; }
        internal set { _member.Entity = value; MemberID = value.MemberID; }
    }
}
```

This code brings up several points:

- This does, to some extent, compromise the purity of the object-oriented domain model. I don't really mind the attributes (e.g., [Column]) because they're not inside any actual code, but you do also have to use EntityRef<T> and EntitySet<T> to store associations between entities. EntityRef<T> and EntitySet<T> are LINQ to SQL's special way of describing references between entities that supports lazy-loading (i.e., fetching the referenced entities from the database only on demand).

- In LINQ to SQL, *every* domain object has to be an entity with a primary key. That means we need an ID value on everything—even on Bid, which shouldn't really need one. Bid is therefore a value object only in the sense that it's immutable. Similarly, any foreign key in the database has to map to a [Column] in the object model, so it's necessary to add ItemID and MemberID to Bid. Fortunately, you can mark such ID values as internal, so it doesn't expose the compromise outside the model layer.

- Instead of using Member.LoginName as a primary key, I've added a new, artificial primary key (MemberID). That will be handy if it's ever necessary to change login names. Again, it can be marked internal, because it's not important to the rest of the application.

- The `Item.Bids` collection returns a list in *read-only* mode. This is vital for proper encapsulation, ensuring that any changes to the `Bids` collection happens via domain model code that can enforce appropriate business rules.

- Even though these classes don't define any domain logic (they're just data containers), they are still the right place to put domain logic (e.g., the `AddBid()` method on `Item`). We just haven't got to that bit yet.

If you want the system to create a corresponding database schema automatically, you can arrange it with a few lines of code:

```
DataContext dc = new DataContext(connectionString); // Open a DataContext
dc.GetTable<Member>(); // Tells dc it's responsible for persisting Member
dc.GetTable<Item>();   // Tells dc it's responsible for persisting Item
dc.GetTable<Bid>();    // Tells dc it's responsible for persisting Bid
dc.CreateDatabase();   // Causes dc to issue a CREATE TABLE for each class
```

Remember, though, that you'll have to perform any future schema updates manually, because `CreateDatabase()` can't update an existing database. Alternatively, create the schema manually in the first place. Either way, once you've created a corresponding database schema, you can create, update, and delete entities using LINQ syntax and methods on `System.Data.Linq.DataContext`. Here's an example of constructing and saving a new entity:

```
DataContext dc = new DataContext(connectionString);
dc.GetTable<Member>().InsertOnSubmit(new Member
{
    LoginName = "Steve",
    ReputationPoints = 0
});
dc.SubmitChanges();
```

And here's an example of retrieving a list of entities in a particular order:

```
DataContext dc = new DataContext(connectionString);
var members = from m in dc.GetTable<Member>()
              orderby m.ReputationPoints descending
              select m;
foreach (Member m in members)
    Console.WriteLine("Name: {0}, Points: {1}",
                      m.LoginName, m.ReputationPoints);
```

You'll learn more about the internal workings of LINQ queries, and the new C# language features that support them, later in this chapter. For now, instead of scattering data access code all over the place, let's implement some repositories.

## Implementing the Auction Repositories

Now that the LINQ to SQL mappings are set up, it's dead easy to provide a full implementation of the repositories outlined earlier:

```
public class MembersRepository
{
    private Table<Member> membersTable;
    public MembersRepository(string connectionString)    {
        membersTable = new DataContext(connectionString)
                       .GetTable<Member>();
    }

    public void AddMember(Member member)
    {
        membersTable.InsertOnSubmit(member);
    }

    public void SubmitChanges()
    {
        membersTable.Context.SubmitChanges();
    }

    public Member FetchByLoginName(string loginName)
```

```csharp
    {
        // If this syntax is unfamiliar to you, check out the explanation
        // of lambda methods near the end of this chapter
        return membersTable.FirstOrDefault(m => m.LoginName == loginName);
    }
}

public class ItemsRepository
{
    private Table<Item> itemsTable;
    public ItemsRepository(string connectionString)
    {
        DataContext dc = new DataContext(connectionString);
        itemsTable = dc.GetTable<Item>();
    }

    public IList<Item> ListItems(int pageSize, int pageIndex)
    {
        return itemsTable.Skip(pageSize * pageIndex)
                        .Take(pageSize).ToList();
    }

    public void SubmitChanges()
    {
        itemsTable.Context.SubmitChanges();
    }

    public void AddItem(Item item)
    {
        itemsTable.InsertOnSubmit(item);
    }

    public Item FetchByID(int itemID)
    {
        return itemsTable.FirstOrDefault(i => i.ItemID == itemID);
    }
}
```

Notice that these repositories take a connection string as a constructor parameter, and then create their own `DataContext` from it. This context-per-repository pattern means that repositories don't interfere with one another, accidentally saving each other's changes or rolling them back. Taking a connection string as a constructor parameter works really well with an IoC container, because you can set up constructor parameters in a configuration file, as you'll see later in the chapter.

Now you can interact with your data store purely through the repository—for example:

```
ItemsRepository itemsRep = new ItemsRepository(connectionString);
itemsRep.AddItem(new Item
{
    Title = "Private Jet",
    AuctionEndDate = new DateTime(2012, 1, 1),
    Description = "Your chance to own a private jet."
});
itemsRep.SubmitChanges();
```

## Building Loosely Coupled Components

One common metaphor in software architecture is *layers* (see Figure 3-6).

*Figure 3-6. A layered architecture*

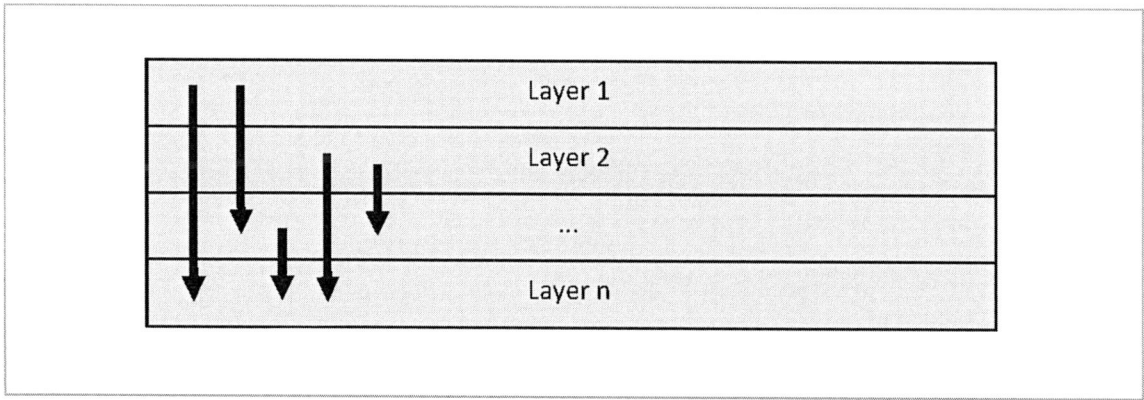

In this architecture, each layer depends only on lower layers, meaning that each layer is only aware of the existence of, and is only able to access, code in the same or lower layers. Typically, the top layer is a UI, middle layers handle domain concerns, and the bottom layers are for data persistence and other shared services. The key benefit is that, when developing code in each layer, you can forget about the implementation of other layers and just think about the API that you're exposing above. This helps you to manage complexity in a large system.

This "layer cake" metaphor is useful, but there are other ways to think about software design, too. Consider the alternative represented in Figure 3-7, in which software pieces are related to components on a circuit board.

*Figure 3-7. The circuit board metaphor for software components*

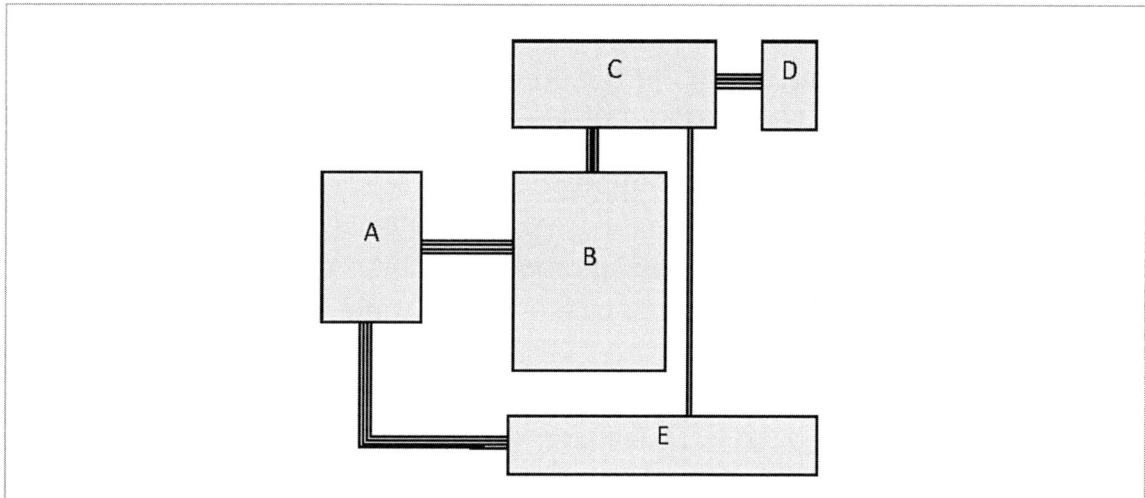

A *component-oriented* design is a little more flexible than a layered design. With this mindset, we don't emphasize the location of each component in a fixed pile, but instead we emphasize that each component is *self-contained*, and communicates with selected others only through a *well-defined interface*.

Components never make any assumptions about the inner workings of any other component: they consider each other component to be a black box that correctly fulfils one or more public contracts (e.g., .NET interfaces), just as the chips on a circuit board don't care for each other's internal mechanisms, but merely interoperate through standard connectors and buses. To prevent careless tight coupling, each software component shouldn't even know of the existence of any other concrete component, but should know only the interface, which expresses functionality but nothing about internal workings. This goes beyond encapsulation; this is *loose coupling*.

For an obvious example, when you need to send e-mail, create an "e-mail sender" component with an abstract interface. You can then attach it to the domain model, or to some other service component (without having to worry about where exactly it fits in the stack), and then easily set up domain model tests using mock implementations of the e-mail sender interface, or in the future swap out the e-mail sender implementation for another if you change your SMTP infrastructure.

Going a step further, repositories are just another type of service component, so you don't really need a special "data access" layer to contain them. It doesn't matter *how* a repository component fulfils requests to load, save, or query data—it just has to satisfy some interface that describes the available operations. As far as its consumers are concerned, any other implementation of the same contract is just as good, whether it stores data in a database, in flat files, across a web service, or anything else. Working against an abstract interface again reinforces the component's separation—not just technically, but also in the minds of the developers implementing its features.

## Taking a Balanced Approach

A component-oriented design isn't mutually exclusive with a layered design (you can have a general sense of layering in your component graph if it helps), and not everything has to expose an abstract interface—for example, your UI probably doesn't need to, because nothing will depend upon it. Similarly, in a small ASP.NET MVC application, you might choose not to completely decouple your controllers from your domain model—it depends on whether there's enough logic in the domain model to warrant maintaining all the interfaces. However, you'll almost certainly benefit by encapsulating data access code and services inside abstract components.

Be flexible; do what works best in each case. The real value is in understanding the mindset: unlike in a pure layered design where each layer tends to be tightly coupled to the one and only concrete implementation of each lower layer, componentization promotes encapsulation and design-by-contract on a piece-by-piece basis, which leads to greater simplicity and testability.

## Using Inversion of Control

Component-oriented design goes hand in hand with IoC. IoC is a software design pattern that helps you decouple your application components from one another. There is one problem with IoC: its name.[19] It sounds like a magic incantation, making developers assume that it's complicated, obscure, or advanced. But it isn't—it's simple, and it's really, really useful. And yes, it can seem a bit odd at first, so let's talk through some examples.

Imagine you have a class, `PasswordResetHelper`, that needs to send e-mail and write to a log file. Without IoC, you *could* allow it to construct concrete instances of `MyEmailSender` and `MyLogWriter`, and use them directly to complete its task. But then you've got hard-coded dependencies from `PasswordResetHelper` to the other two components, leaking and weaving their specific concerns and API designs throughout `PasswordResetHelper`. You can't then design and test `PasswordResetHelper` in isolation, and of course switching to a different e-mail-sending or log-writing technology will involve considerable changes to `PasswordResetHelper`. The three classes are fused together. That's the starting point for the dreaded spaghetti code disease.

---

[19] The other common term for it is *dependency injection (DI)*, which sounds less pretentious to me, but *IoC* is more commonly used, so we'll stick with that.

Avoid this by applying the IoC pattern. Factor out interfaces that describe arbitrary e-mail-sending and log-writing components (e.g., `IEmailSender` and `ILogWriter`), and then make `PasswordResetHelper` dependent only on those interfaces:

```
public class PasswordResetHelper
{
    private IEmailSender _emailSender;
    private ILogWriter _logWriter;

    // Constructor
    public PasswordResetHelper(IEmailSender emailSender,
                              ILogWriter logWriter)
    {
        // This is the Inversion-of-Control bit. The constructor demands
        // instances of IEmailSender and ILogWriter, which we save and
        // will use later.
        this._emailSender = emailSender;
        this._logWriter = logWriter;
    }

    // Rest of code uses _emailSender and _logWriter
}
```

Now, `PasswordResetHelper` needs no knowledge of any specific concrete e-mail sender or log writer. It knows and cares *only* about the interfaces, which could equally well describe any e-mail-sending or log-writing technology, without getting bogged down in the concerns of any specific one. You can easily switch to a different concrete implementation (e.g., for a different technology), or support multiple ones concurrently, without changing `PasswordResetHelper`. In unit tests, as you'll see later, you can supply mock implementations that allow for simple tests, or ones that simulate particular external circumstances (e.g., error conditions). You have achieved loose coupling.

The name *Inversion of Control* comes from the fact that external code (i.e., whatever instantiates `PasswordResetHelper`) gets to control which concrete implementations of its dependencies it uses. That's the inverse of the normal situation, in which `PasswordResetHelper` would control its choice of concrete classes to depend upon.

## An MVC-Specific Example

Let's go back to the auctions example, and apply IoC. The specific goal is to create a controller class, `AdminController`, that uses the LINQ to SQL–powered `MembersRepository`, but without coupling `AdminController` to `MembersRepository` (with all its LINQ to SQL and database connection string concerns).

We'll start by assuming that you've refactored the `MembersRepository` to implement a `public interface`:

```
public interface IMembersRepository
{
    void AddMember(Member member);
    Member FetchByLoginName(string loginName);
    void SubmitChanges();
}
```

(Of course, you still have the concrete `MembersRepository` class that now implements this interface.) You can now write an ASP.NET MVC controller class that depends on `IMembersRepository`:

```
public class AdminController : Controller
{
    IMembersRepository membersRepository;

    // Constructor
    public AdminController(IMembersRepository membersRepository)
    {
        this.membersRepository = membersRepository;
    }

    public ActionResult ChangeLoginName(string oldLogin, string newLogin)
    {
        Member member = membersRepository.FetchByLoginName(oldLogin);
        member.LoginName = newLogin;
        membersRepository.SubmitChanges();

        // ... now render some view
    }
}
```

This AdminController requires you to supply an implementation of
IMembersRepository as a constructor parameter. Now, AdminController can
just work with the IMembersRepository interface, and doesn't need to know
of any concrete implementation.

This simplifies AdminController in several ways—for one thing, it no longer
needs to know or care about database connection strings (remember, the
concrete MembersRepository demands connectionString as a constructor
parameter). The bigger benefit is that IoC ensures that you're coding to
contract (i.e., explicit interfaces), and it greatly enhances testability (we'll
create an automated test for ChangeLoginName() in a moment).

But wait a minute—something further up the call stack now has to
instantiate a MembersRepository—so that now needs to supply a
connectionString. Does IoC really help, or does it just move the problem
from one place to another? What if you have loads of components and
dependencies, and even chains of dependencies with child dependencies—

how will you manage all this, and won't the end result just be even more complicated? Say hello to the *IoC container*.

## Using an IoC Container

An IoC container is a standard software component that supports and simplifies IoC. It lets you register a set of components (i.e., abstract types and your currently chosen concrete implementations), and then handles the business of instantiating them. You can configure and register components either with an XML file or with C# code (or both).

At runtime, you can call a method similar to `container.Resolve(Type type)`, where `type` could be a particular `interface` or `abstract` type or a particular concrete type, and the container will return an object satisfying that type definition, according to whatever concrete type is configured. It sounds trivial, but a good IoC container adds three extra clever features:

- *Dependency chain resolution*: If you request a component that itself has dependencies (e.g., constructor parameters), the container will satisfy those dependencies recursively, so you can have component A, which depends on B, which depends on C, and so on. In other words, you can forget about the wiring on your component circuit board: just think about the components, because wiring happens magically.

- *Object lifetime management*: If you request component A more than once, should you get the same actual instance of A each time, or a fresh new instance each time? The container will usually let you configure the "lifestyle" of a component, selecting from predefined options including singleton (the same instance each time), transient (a new instance each time), instance-per-thread, instance-from-a-pool, and so on.

- *Configure explicit constructor parameter values*: For example, if the constructor for `MembersRepository` demands a string called `connectionString` (as ours did earlier), you can configure a value for it in your XML config file. It's a crude but simple configuration system that removes any need for your code to pass around connection strings, SMTP server addresses, and so on.

So, in the preceding example, you'd configure `MembersRepository` as the active concrete implementation for `IMembersRepository`. Then, when some code calls `container.Resolve(typeof(AdminController))`, the container will figure out from the constructor parameters that it first needs an `IMembersRepository`, will get one according to whatever concrete implementation you've configured (i.e., `MembersRepository`), supplying the `connectionString` you've configured, and will use that to instantiate and return an `AdminController`.

## Meet Castle Windsor

Castle Windsor is a popular open source IoC container. It has all these features and works well in ASP.NET MVC. So, you supply a configuration that maps abstract types (interfaces) to specific concrete types, and then when someone calls `myWindsorInstance.Resolve<ISomeAbstractType>()`, it will return an instance of whatever corresponding concrete type is currently configured, resolving any chain of dependencies and respecting your component's configured lifestyle.

This is especially useful in ASP.NET MVC for building a "controller factory" that can resolve dependencies automatically. Continuing the previous example, this means that `AdminController`'s dependency on `IMembersRepository` will be resolved automatically, according to whatever concrete implementation you've currently got configured for `IMembersRepository`.

Here's an example of an `IControllerFactory` that uses Windsor to instantiate controllers:

```
public class WindsorControllerFactory : IControllerFactory
{
  IWindsorContainer container;
  public WindsorControllerFactory()
  {
    container = new WindsorContainer(
                new XmlInterpreter(new ConfigResource("myConfigSection"))
            );

    // Don't expect all controllers to be listed in the XML file
    // Just find them in the running assembly
    container.Register(AllTypes.Of<IController>()
                .FromAssembly(Assembly.GetExecutingAssembly())
                .Configure(component => component.LifeStyle.Transient
                            .Named(component.Implementation.Name)
            ));
  }

  // Called at the start of each request to resolve a controller
  public IController CreateController(RequestContext ctx,
                                    string controllerName)
  {
    // ASP.NET MVC's convention is to append "Controller"
    // to controller names
    string name = controllerName + "Controller";
    return container.Resolve<IController>(name);
  }

  public void DisposeController(IController controller)
```

```
  {
    IDisposable disp = controller as IDisposable;
    if (disp != null)
      disp.Dispose();
  }
}
```

ASP.NET MVC provides an easy means for hooking up a custom controller factory—you just need to add an `Application_Start` handler to your `Global.asax.cs` file, like so:

```
protected void Application_Start()
{
    ControllerBuilder.Current.SetControllerFactory(
        new WindsorControllerFactory()
    );
}
```

The IoC container's dependency chain resolution feature will then take care of hooking up whatever components are needed to service each request.

## Getting Started with Automated Testing

In recent years, automated testing has turned from a minority interest into a mainstream, can't-live-without-it, core development technique. The ASP.NET MVC Framework is designed, from every possible angle, to make it as easy as possible to set up unit tests and integration tests. When you create a brand-new ASP.NET MVC web application project, Visual Studio even prompts you to help set up a unit testing project, offering project templates for multiple testing frameworks.

In the .NET world, you can choose from a range of open source and commercial unit test frameworks, the most widely known of which is NUnit. Typically, you create a separate class library project in your solution to hold *test fixtures* (unless Visual Studio has already created one for you). A test fixture is a C# class that defines a set of test methods—one test method per behavior that you want to verify. Here's an example test

fixture, written using NUnit, that tests the behavior of
AdminController.ChangeLoginName() from the previous example:

```
[TestFixture]
public class AdminControllerTests
{
    [Test]
    public void Can_Change_Login_Name()
    {
        // Arrange (Set up a scenario)
        Member bob = new Member { LoginName = "Bob" };
        FakeMembersRepository repos = new FakeMembersRepository();
        repos.Members.Add(bob);
        AdminController controller = new AdminController(repos);

        // Act (Attempt the operation)
        controller.ChangeLoginName("Bob", "Anastasia");

        // Assert (Verify the result)
        Assert.AreEqual("Anastasia", bob.LoginName);
        Assert.IsTrue(repos.DidSubmitChanges);
    }

    private class FakeMembersRepository : IMembersRepository
    {
        public List<Member> Members = new List<Member>();
        public bool DidSubmitChanges = false;

        public void AddMember(Member member) {
            throw new NotImplementedException();
        }

        public Member FetchByLoginName(string loginName)
        {
            return Members.First(m => m.LoginName == loginName);
        }

        public void SubmitChanges()
```

```
        {
            DidSubmitChanges = true;
        }
    }
}
```

This test fixture uses a test-specific fake implementation of
IMembersRepository to simulate a particular condition (i.e., there's one
member in the repository: Bob). Next, it calls the method being tested
(ChangeLoginName()), and finally verifies the result using a series of
Assert() calls. You can run your tests using one of many freely available
test runner GUIs,[20] such as NUnit GUI (see Figure 3-8).

*Figure 3-8. NUnit GUI showing a green light*

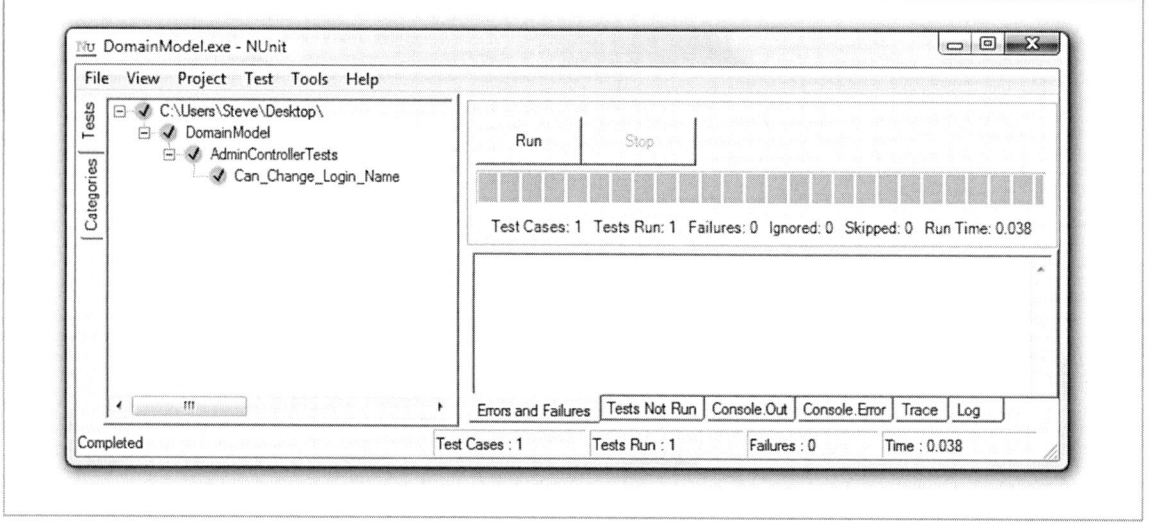

*NUnit GUI* finds all the [TestFixture] classes in an assembly, and all their
[Test] methods, letting you run them either individually or all in sequence.
If all the Assert() calls pass, and no unexpected exceptions are thrown,

---

[20] And if you have a build server (e.g., if you use continuous integration), you can run such automated
tests using a command-line tool as part of the build process.

you'll get a green light. Otherwise, you'll get a red light and a list of which assertions failed.

It might seem like a lot of code to verify a simple behavior, but it wouldn't be much more code even if you were testing a very complex behavior.

## Unit Tests and Integration Tests

The preceding test is a *unit test*, because it tests just one isolated component: `AdminController`. It doesn't rely on any real implementation of `IMembersRepository`, and so it doesn't need to access any database.

Things would be different if `AdminController` wasn't so well decoupled from its dependencies. If, instead, it directly referenced a concrete `MembersRepository`, which in turn contained database access code, then it would be impossible to test `AdminController` in isolation—you'd be forced to test the repository, the data access code, and even the SQL database itself all at once. That's not ideal, because

- It's slow. When you have hundreds of tests, and you're waiting for them all to do a series of database queries or web service calls, have a good book handy.

- You can get false negatives. Maybe the database was momentarily down for some reason, but now you're convinced there's an intermittent bug in your code.

- You can even get false positives. Two components might accidentally cancel out each other's bugs. Honestly, it happens!

When you deliberately chain together a series of components and test them together, that's an *integration test*. These are valuable, too, because they prove that the whole stack (including database mappings) is working properly. But for the aforementioned reasons, you'll get best results by concentrating on unit tests, and just adding a few integration tests to check the overall integration.

# The Red-Green Development Style

You're off to a good start with automated testing. But how do you know whether your tests actually prove something? What if you accidentally missed out a vital `Assert()`, or didn't set up your simulated conditions quite right, so that the test gives a false positive? *Red-green development* is an approach to writing code that implicitly "tests your tests." The basic workflow is as follows:

1. Decide that you need to add a new behavior to your code. Write a unit test for the behavior, even though you haven't implemented it yet.

2. See the test fail (red).

3. Implement the behavior.

4. See the test pass (green).

5. Repeat.

The fact that the test result switches from red to green, even though you don't change the test, proves that it responds to the behavior you've added in the code.

Let's see an example. Earlier in this chapter, during the auctions example, there was planned to be a method on `Item` called `AddBid()`, but we haven't implemented it yet. Let's say the behavior we want is "You can add bids to an item, but any new bid must be higher than all previous bids." First, add a method stub to the `Item` class:

```
public void AddBid(Member fromMember, decimal bidAmount)
{
    throw new NotImplementedException();
}
```

It may be obvious that this code doesn't satisfy the desired behavior, but that doesn't stop you writing a test:

```
[TestFixture]
public class AuctionItemTests
```

```
{
    [Test]
    public void Can_Add_Bid()
    {
        // Set up a scenario
        Member member = new Member();
        Item item = new Item();

        // Attempt the operation
        item.AddBid(member, 150);

        // Verify the result
        Assert.AreEqual(1, item.Bids.Count());
        Assert.AreEqual(150, item.Bids[0].BidAmount);
        Assert.AreSame(member, item.Bids[0].Member);
    }
}
```

Run this test, and of course you'll get a red light (NotImplementedException).
It's time to create a first-draft implementation for Item.AddBid():

```
public void AddBid(Member fromMember, decimal bidAmount)
{
    _bids.Add(new Bid
    {
        Member = fromMember,
        BidAmount = bidAmount,
        DatePlaced = DateTime.Now,
        ItemID = this.ItemID
    });
}
```

Now if you run the test again, you'll get a green light. So, this proves you
can add bids, but says nothing about new bids being higher than existing
ones. Start the red-green cycle again by adding two more tests:

```
[Test]
public void Can_Add_Higher_Bid()
{
    // Set up a scenario
    Member member1 = new Member();
    Member member2 = new Member();
    Item item = new Item();

    // Attempt the operation
    item.AddBid(member1, 150);
    item.AddBid(member2, 200);

    // Verify the result
    Assert.AreEqual(2, item.Bids.Count());
    Assert.AreEqual(150, item.Bids[0].BidAmount);
    Assert.AreEqual(200, item.Bids[1].BidAmount);
    Assert.AreSame(member1, item.Bids[0].Member);
    Assert.AreSame(member2, item.Bids[1].Member);
}

[Test]
public void Cannot_Add_Lower_Bid()
{
    // Set up a scenario
    Member member1 = new Member();
    Member member2 = new Member();
    Item item = new Item();

    // Attempt the operation
    item.AddBid(member1, 150);
    try
    {
        item.AddBid(member2, 100);
        Assert.Fail("Should throw exception when invalid bid attempted");
    }
    catch (InvalidOperationException) { /* Expected */ }

    // Verify the result
    Assert.AreEqual(1, item.Bids.Count());
    Assert.AreEqual(150, item.Bids[0].BidAmount);
    Assert.AreSame(member1, item.Bids[0].Member);
}
```

Run all three tests together, and you'll see that Can_Add_Bid and Can_Add_Higher_Bid both pass, whereas Cannot_Add_Lower_Bid fails (showing, as in Figure 3-9, that the test correctly detects a failure to prevent adding lower bids).

**Figure 3-9. NUnit GUI shows that we failed to prevent adding lower bids.**

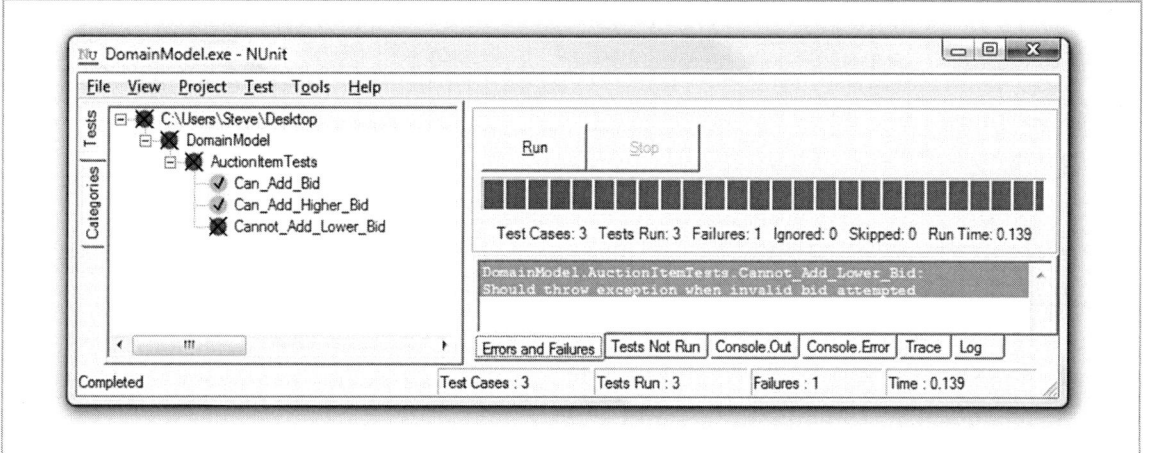

Of course, there isn't yet any code to prevent you from adding lower bids. Update Item.AddBid():

```
public void AddBid(Member fromMember, decimal bidAmount)
{
    if ((Bids.Count() > 0) && (bidAmount <= Bids.Max(b => b.BidAmount)))
        throw new InvalidOperationException("Bid too low");
    else
    {
        _bids.Add(new Bid
        {
            Member = fromMember,
            BidAmount = bidAmount,
            DatePlaced = DateTime.Now,
            ItemID = this.ItemID
        });
    }
}
```

Run the tests again, and all three will pass! And that, in a nutshell, is red-green development. The tests must prove something, because their outcome changes when you implement the corresponding behavior. If you want to take this a step further, define behaviors for error cases, too (e.g., when `Member` is `null` or `bidAmount` is negative), write tests for those, and then implement the behaviors.

### So, Was It Worth It?

Writing tests certainly means you have to do more typing, but it ensures the code's behavior is now "locked down" forever—nobody's going to break this code without noticing it, and you can refactor to your heart's content, and then get rapid reassurance that the whole code base still works properly. Personally, I love being able to do long stretches of work on my domain model, controllers, or service classes, testing behavior as I go, without ever having to fire up a web browser. It's faster, and you can test edge cases that would be very difficult to simulate manually through the application's UI. Adding in the red-green iterative development style might seem to increase your workload further, but does it really? If you're going to write the tests anyway, why not write them first?

Red-green development is the central idea in TDD. TDD proponents use the red-green cycle for each change they make to the software, and then when all tests pass, refactor to keep code quality high. Ultimately, the theory is that a suite of tests completely defines and documents the behavior of an entire application, although it's generally accepted that some software components, notably views and client-side code in web development, can't always be tested this way.

ASP.NET MVC is specifically designed to maximize testability. `Controller` classes aren't coupled to the HTTP runtime—they access `Request`, `Response`, and other context objects only through abstract interfaces, so you can replace them with fake or mock versions during tests. By instantiating controllers through an IoC container, you can hook them up to any graph of loosely coupled components.

## Summary

In this chapter, you got up to speed with the core concepts underpinning ASP.NET MVC, and the tools and techniques needed for successful web development with the latest .NET 3.5 technologies.

# Appendix: New C# 3 Language Features

In this appendix, you'll learn about the innovative new language features that Microsoft added to C# with .NET 3.5 and the Visual Studio 2008 ("Orcas") release in November 2007. If you already know all about LINQ, anonymous types, lambda methods, and so on, you can safely skip it. Otherwise, you'll need this knowledge before you can really understand what's going on in an ASP.NET MVC application. I'll assume you already understand C# 2, including generics, iterators (i.e., the `yield return` statement), and anonymous delegates.

## The Design Goal: Language Integrated Query

Almost all the new language features in C# 3 have one thing in common: they exist to support LINQ. The idea of LINQ is to make data querying a native feature of the language, so that when you're selecting, sorting, filtering, or transforming of sets of data—whether it's a set of .NET objects in memory, a set of XML nodes in a file on disk, or a set of rows in a SQL database—you can do so using one standard, IntelliSense-assisted syntax in your C# code (and using far less code).

As a very simple example, in C# 2, if you wanted to find the top three integers in an array, you'd write a function like this:

```csharp
int[] GetTopThreeValues(int[] values)
{
    Array.Sort(values);
    int[] topThree = new int[3];
    for (int i = 0; i < 3; i++)
        topThree[i] = values[values.Length - i - 1];
    return topThree;
}
```

whereas using LINQ, you'd simply write this:

```csharp
var topThree = (from i in values orderby i descending select i).Take(3);
```

Note that the C# 2 code has the unfortunate side effect of destroying the original sort order of the array—it's slightly trickier if you want to avoid that. The LINQ code does not have this problem.

At first, it's hard to imagine how this strange, SQL-like syntax actually works, especially when you consider that much more complex LINQ queries might join, group, and filter heterogeneous data sources. Let's consider each one of the underlying mechanisms in turn, not just to help you understand LINQ, but also because those mechanisms turn out to be useful programming tools in their own right, and you need to understand their syntax to use ASP.NET MVC effectively.

## Extension Methods

Have you ever wanted to add an extra method onto a class you don't own? Extension methods give you the syntactic convenience of "adding" methods to arbitrary classes, even sealed ones, without letting you access their private members or otherwise compromising on encapsulation.

For example, a string doesn't by default have a method to convert itself to title case (in which the first letter of each word is capitalized), so you might traditionally define a static method to do it:

```
public static string ToTitleCase(string str)
{
    if (str == null)
        return null;
    else
        return CultureInfo.CurrentUICulture.TextInfo.ToTitleCase(str);
}
```

Now, by placing this static method in a public static class, and by using the this keyword in the parameter list, as in the following code

```
public static class MyExtensions
{
    public static string ToTitleCase(this string str)
    {
        if (str == null)
            return null;
        else
            return CultureInfo.CurrentUICulture.TextInfo.ToTitleCase(str);
    }
}
```

you have created an *extension method* (i.e., a `static` method that takes a
`this` parameter). The C# compiler lets you call it as if it were a method on
the .NET type corresponding to the `this` parameter—for example

```
string place = "south west australia";
Console.WriteLine(place.ToTitleCase()); // Prints "South West Australia"
```

Of course, this is fully recognized by Visual Studio's IntelliSense. Note
that it doesn't *really* add an extra method to the `string` class. It's just a
syntactic convenience: the C# compiler actually converts your code into
something looking almost exactly like the first nonextension static method
in the preceding code, so there's no way you can violate any member
protection or encapsulation rules this way.

There's nothing to stop you from defining an extension method on an
interface, which creates the previously impossible illusion of having code
automatically shared by all implementers of an interface. The following
example uses the C# 2 `yield return` keyword to get all the even values out
of an `IEnumerable<int>`:

```
public static class MyExtensions
{
    public static IEnumerable<int> WhereEven(this IEnumerable<int> values)
    {
        foreach (int i in values)
            if (i % 2 == 0)
                yield return i;
    }
}
```

You'll now find that `WhereEven()` is available on `List<int>`, `Collection<int>`, `int[]`, and anything else that implements `IEnumerable<int>`.

## Lambda Methods

If you wanted to generalize the preceding `WhereEven()` function into an arbitrary `Where<T>()` function, performing an arbitrary filter on an arbitrary data type, you could use a delegate, like so:

```
public static class MyExtensions
{
    public delegate bool Criteria<T>(T value);
    public static IEnumerable<T> Where<T>(this IEnumerable<T> values,
                                          Criteria<T> criteria)
    {
        foreach (T item in values)
            if (criteria(item))
                yield return item;
    }
}
```

Now you could, for example, use `Where<T>` to get all the strings in an array that start with a particular letter, by passing a C# 2 anonymous delegate for its `criteria` parameter:

```
string[] names = new string[] { "Bill", "Jane", "Bob", "Frank" };
IEnumerable<string> Bs = names.Where<string>(
                            delegate(string s) { return s.StartsWith("B"); }
                         );
```

I think you'll agree that this is starting to look quite ugly. That's why C# 3 introduces *lambda methods* (well, borrows them from functional programming languages), which is a simplified syntax for writing anonymous delegates. The preceding code may be reduced to

```
string[] names = new string[] { "Bill", "Jane", "Bob", "Frank" };
IEnumerable<string> Bs = names.Where<string>(s => s.StartsWith("B"));
```

That's much tidier, and even starts to read a bit like an English sentence. In general, lambda methods let you express a delegate with any number of parameters using the following syntax:

```
(a, b, c) => SomeFunctionOf(a, b, c)
```

If you're describing a delegate that takes only one parameter, you can drop the first set of parentheses:

```
x => SomeFunctionOf(x)
```

Once again, this is just a compiler feature, so you're able to use lambda methods when calling into a .NET 2.0 assembly that expects a delegate.

## Generic Type Inference

Actually, the previous example can be made one step simpler:

```
string[] names = new string[] { "Bill", "Jane", "Bob", "Frank" };
IEnumerable<string> Bs = names.Where(s => s.StartsWith("B"));
```

Spot the difference. This time, we haven't specified the generic parameter for `Where<T>()`—we just wrote `Where()`. That's another one of the C# 3 compiler's party tricks: it can infer the type of a function's generic argument from the return type of a delegate (or lambda method) passed to it. (The C# 2 compiler had some generic type inference abilities, but it couldn't do this.)

Now we have a totally general purpose `Where()` operator with a tidy syntax, which is a long way toward understanding how LINQ works.

## Automatic Properties

This will seem like a strange tangent in this discussion, but bear with me. Most of us C# programmers are, by now, quite bored of writing properties like this:

```
private string _name;
public string Name
{
    get { return _name; }
    set { _name = value; }
}

private int _age;
public int Age
{
    get { return _age; }
    set { _age = value; }
}

// ... and so on
```

So much code, so little reward. It makes you tempted just to expose a
public field on your class, considering that the end result is the same, but
that prevents you from ever adding getter or setter logic in the future
without breaking compatibility with assemblies you've already shipped
(and screws up data binding). Fortunately, our hero the C# 3 compiler is
back with a new syntax:

```
public string Name { get; set; }
public int Age { get; set; }
```

These are known as *automatic properties*. During compilation, the C# 3
compiler automatically adds a private *backing field* for each automatic
property (with a weird name you'll never access directly), and wires up the
obvious getters and setters. So now you have the benefits, but without the
pain. Note that you can't omit the `get;` or `set;` clauses to create a read-only
or write-only field; you add an access modifier instead—for example

```
public string Name { get; private set; }
public int Age { internal get; set; }
```

Should you need to add custom getter or setter logic in the future, you can
convert these to regular properties without breaking compatibility with
anything. There's a missing feature, though—there's no way to assign a

default value to an automatic property as you can with a field (e.g., `private object myObject = new object();`), so you have to initialize them during your constructor, if at all.

## Object and Collection Initializers

Here's another common programming task that's quite boring: constructing objects, and then assigning values to their properties. For example

```
Person person = new Person();
person.Name = "Steve";
person.Age = 93;
RegisterPerson(person);
```

It's one simple task, but it takes four lines of code to implement it. Just when you were on the brink of getting RSI, the C# 3 compiler swoops in with a new syntax:

```
RegisterPerson(new Person { Name = "Steve", Age = 93 });
```

So much better! By using the curly brace notation after a `new`, you can assign values to the new object's publicly settable properties, which is great when you're just creating a quick new instance to pass into a method. The code within the curly braces is called an *object initializer*, and you can put it after a normal set of constructor parameters if you need. Or, if you're calling a parameterless constructor, you can simply omit the normal constructor parentheses.

Along similar lines, the C# 3 compiler will generate some code for you if you're initializing a new collection. For example

```
List<string> countries = new List<string>();
countries.Add("England");
countries.Add("Ireland");
countries.Add("Scotland");
countries.Add("Wales");
```

can now be reduced to

```
List<string> countries = new List<string> {
    "England", "Ireland", "Scotland", "Wales"
};
```

The compiler lets you use this syntax when constructing any type that exposes a method called Add(). There's a corresponding syntax for initializing dictionaries, too:

```
Dictionary<int, string> zipCodes = new Dictionary<int,string> {
    { 90210, "Beverly Hills" },
    { 73301, "Austin, TX" }
};
```

## Type Inference

C# 3 also introduces the var keyword, in which a local variable is defined without specifying an explicit type—the compiler infers the type from the value being assigned to it. For examplew

```
var now = new DateTime(2001, 1, 1); // The variable takes the type DateTime
int dayOfYear = now.DayOfYear;      // This is legal
string test = now.Substring(1, 3);  // Error! No such function on DateTime
```

This is called *type inference* or *implicit typing*. Note that, although many developers misunderstand this point at first, *it's not a dynamically typed variable* (e.g., in the sense that all variables are dynamically typed in JavaScript). After compilation, it's just as explicitly typed as ever—the only difference is that the compiler works out what type it should be instead of being told. Implicitly typed variables can only be used in a local method scope: you can't use var for a class member or as a return type.

## Anonymous Types

An interesting thing happens at this point. By combining object initializers with type inference, you can construct simple data storage objects without ever having to define a corresponding class anywhere. For example

```
var salesData = new { Day = new DateTime(2009, 01, 03),
                      DollarValue = 353000 };
Console.WriteLine("In {0}, we sold {1:c}", salesData.Day,
                                    salesData.DollarValue);
```

Here, salesData is an *anonymously typed object*. Again, that doesn't mean
it's dynamically typed; it's of some real .NET type that you just don't
happen to know (or care about) the name of. The C# 3 compiler will
generate an invisible class definition on your behalf during compilation.
Note that Visual Studio's IntelliSense is fully aware of what's going on
here, and will pop up the appropriate property list when you type
salesData., even though the type it's prompting you about doesn't even
exist yet. Clever stuff indeed.

The compiler generates a different class definition for each combination of
property names and types that you use to build anonymously typed objects.
So, if two anonymously typed objects have the same property names and
types, then at runtime they'll actually be of the same .NET type. This
means you can put corresponding anonymously typed objects into an
anonymously typed array—for example

```
var dailySales = new[] {
    new { Day = new DateTime(2009, 01, 03), DollarValue = 353000 },
    new { Day = new DateTime(2009, 01, 04), DollarValue = 379250 },
    new { Day = new DateTime(2009, 01, 05), DollarValue = 388200 }
};
```

For this to be allowed, all the anonymously typed objects in the array must
have the same combination of property names and types. Notice that
dailySales is still introduced with the var keyword, never var[] or
List<var> or anything like that. Because var means "whatever fits," it's
always sufficient on its own, and retains full type safety both at compile
time and runtime.

# Putting It All Together

If you haven't seen any of these features before, the last few pages probably seemed quite bizarre, and it might not be obvious how any of this contributes to LINQ. But actually, the scene is now set and all can be revealed.

You've already seen how one might implement a `Where()` operator using extension methods, lambda methods, and generic type inference. The next big step is to show how implicitly typed variables and anonymous types support a *projection* operator (i.e., the equivalent to the SELECT part of a SQL query). The idea with projection is that, for each element in the source set, we want to map it to a transformed element to go into the destination set. In C# 2 terms, you'd use a generic delegate to map each element, like this:

```
public delegate TDest Transformation<TSrc, TDest>(TSrc item);
```

But in C# 3 you can use the built-in delegate type `Func<TSrc, TDest>`, which is exactly equivalent. So, here's a general purpose projection operator:

```
public static class MyExtensions
{
    public static IEnumerable<TDest> Select<T, TDest>
        (this IEnumerable<T> values, Func<T, TDest> transformation)
    {
        foreach (T item in values)
            yield return transformation(item);
    }
}
```

Now, given that both `Select<T, TDest>()` and `Where<T>()` are available on any `IEnumerable<T>`, you can perform an arbitrary filtering and mapping of data onto an anonymously typed collection:

```
// Prepare sample data
string[] nameData = new string[] { "Steve", "Jimmy", "Celine", "Arno" };

// Transform onto an enumerable of anonymously typed objects
var people = nameData.Where(str => str != "Jimmy") // Filter out Jimmy
                .Select(str => new {             // Project to anon type
                    Name = str,
                    LettersInName = str.Length,
                    HasLongName = (str.Length > 5)
                });

// Retrieve data from the enumerable
foreach (var person in people)
    Console.WriteLine("{0} has {1} letters in their name. {2}",
                    person.Name,
                    person.LettersInName,
                    person.HasLongName ? "That's long!" : ""
                );
```

This will print the following to the console:

```
Steve has 5 letters in their name.
Celine has 6 letters in their name. That's long!
Arno has 4 letters in their name.
```

Note that we're assigning the results of the query to an implicitly typed (var) variable. That's because the real type is an enumerable of anonymously typed objects, so there's no way of writing its type explicitly (but the compiler can do so during compilation).

Hopefully it's clear by now that, with Select() and Where(), this could be the basis for a general purpose object query language. No doubt you could also implement OrderBy(), Join(), GroupBy(), and so on. But of course you don't have to, because that's exactly what LINQ to Objects already is—a general purpose query language for in-memory collections of .NET objects, built almost exactly along the lines shown here.

# Deferred Execution

One final point before we move on. Since all the code used to build these query operators uses the C# 2.0 `yield return` keyword, the enumerables don't actually get evaluated until you start enumerating over them. That is, when we instantiated `var people` in the previous example, it defined the nature and parameters of the query (as a closure in memory), but didn't actually touch the data source (`nameData`) until the subsequent `foreach` loop pulled out the results one by one.

This is more than just a theoretical point. It makes a great difference when you're composing and combining queries, and especially when you query an external SQL database, to know that the expensive bit doesn't actually happen until the last possible moment.

# Using LINQ to Objects

So, we're finally here. You've now seen essentially how LINQ to Objects works, and using the various new C# 3 features, you could pretty much reinvent it yourself if you had to. You could certainly add extra general purpose query operators if they turned out to be useful.

When Microsoft's LINQ team got this far, they organized some usability testing, had a beer, and considered their work finished. But predictably, early adopters were still not satisfied. The feedback was that the syntax was still too complicated, and why didn't it just look like SQL? All the dots and brackets were giving people a headache. So, the LINQ crew got back to business and designed a more expressive syntax for the same queries. The previous example could now be reexpressed as

```
var people = from str in nameData
             where str != "Jimmy"
             select new
             {
                 Name = str,
                 LettersInName = str.Length,
                 HasLongName = (str.Length > 5)
             };
```

This new syntax is called a *query expression*. It's an alternative to writing chains of LINQ extension methods, as long as your query follows a prescribed structure. It's very reminiscent of SQL, except that select comes at the end instead of the beginning (which makes more sense when you think about it).

It doesn't make much difference in this example, but query expressions are arguably easier to read than chains of extension methods if you have a longer query with many clauses and subclauses. It's entirely up to you which syntax you choose to use—it makes no difference at runtime, considering that the C# 3 compiler simply converts query expressions into a chain of extension method calls early in the compilation process anyway. Personally, I find some queries easier to express as a chain of function calls, and others look nicer as query expressions, so I swap back and forth between the two.

---

**Note**    In query expression syntax, the keywords (from, where, orderby, select, etc.) are hard-coded into the language. You can't add your own keywords. There are lots of LINQ extension methods that are only reachable by calling them directly, because there's no corresponding query expression keyword. You can of course use extension method calls inside a query expression (e.g., from p in people.Distinct() orderby p.Name select p).

---

# Lambda Expressions

The final new C# 3 compiler feature isn't something you'll want to involve in all your code, but it creates powerful new possibilities for API designers. It's the basis for LINQ to Everything, as well as some of the ingeniously expressive APIs in ASP.NET MVC.

*Lambda expressions* look just like lambda methods—the syntax is identical—but during compilation they aren't converted into anonymous delegates. Instead, they're embedded in the assembly as *data*, not code, called an *abstract syntax tree (AST)*. Here's an example:

```
// This is a regular lambda method and is compiled to .NET code
Func<int, int, int> add1 = (x, y) => x + y;

// This is a lambda expression and is compiled to *data* (an AST)
Expression<Func<int, int, int>> add2 = (x, y) => x + y;

// You can compile the expression *at runtime* then run it
Console.WriteLine("1 + 2 = " + add2.Compile()(1, 2));

// Or, at runtime, you can inspect it as a hierarchy of expressions
Console.WriteLine("Root node type: " + add2.Body.NodeType.ToString());
BinaryExpression rootNode = add2.Body as BinaryExpression;
Console.WriteLine("LHS: " + rootNode.Left.NodeType.ToString());
Console.WriteLine("RHS: " + rootNode.Right.NodeType.ToString());
```

This will output the following:

```
1 + 2 = 3
Root node type: Add
LHS: Parameter
RHS: Parameter
```

So, merely by adding Expression<> around the delegate type, add2 becomes a data structure that you can do two different things with at runtime:

- Compile into an executable delegate simply by calling `add2.Compile()`
- Inspect as a hierarchy of expressions (here, it's a single `Add` node taking two parameters)

What's more, you can manipulate the expression tree data at runtime, and then still compile it to executable code.

But why on earth would you want to do any of this? It's not just an opportunity to write bizarre, self-modifying code that confuses the heck out of your coworkers (although that is an option). The main purpose is to let you pass code as a parameter into an API method—not to have that code executed, but to communicate some other intention. For example, ASP.NET MVC's `Html.ActionLink<T>` method takes a parameter of type `Expression<Action<T>>`. You call it like this:

```
Html.ActionLink<HomeController>(c => c.Index())
```

The lambda expression gets compiled into a hierarchy consisting of a single `MethodCall` node, specifying the method and parameters you've referenced. ASP.NET MVC doesn't compile and run the expression; it just uses it to figure out which controller and action you're referencing, and then computes the corresponding URL (according to your routing configuration) and returns an HTML hyperlink pointing to that URL.

This syntax, `Html.ActionLink<HomeController>(c => c.Index())`, has the considerable advantage over its more obvious string-based alternative, `Html.ActionLink("Index", "Home")`, that it's more strongly typed and gives you full IntelliSense. It would be impossible without lambda expressions.

## IQueryable<T> and LINQ to SQL

Now that you have lambda expressions, you can do some seriously clever things. There's an important new standard interface in .NET 3.5 called `IQueryable<T>`. It represents deferred-execution queries that can be compiled at runtime not just to executable .NET code but—theoretically— to anything. Most famously, the LINQ to SQL framework component (included in .NET 3.5) provides `IQueryable<T>` objects that it can convert to SQL queries. In your code, you have something like this:

```
var members = (from m in myDataContext.GetTable<Member>()
               where m.LoginName == "Joey"
               select m).ToList();
```

This issues a parameterized (yes, SQL injection–proof) database query as follows:

```
SELECT [t0].[MemberID], [t0].[LoginName], [t0].[ReputationPoints]
FROM [dbo].[Members] AS [t0]
WHERE [t0].[LoginName] = @p0
{Params: @p0 = 'Joey'}
```

So, how does it work? To get started, let's break that single line of C# code into three parts:

```
// [1] Get an IQueryable to represent a database table
IQueryable<Member> membersTable = myDataContext.GetTable<Member>();

// [2] Convert the first IQueryable into a different one by
//     prepending its lambda expression with a Where() node
IQueryable<Member> query1 = membersTable.Where(m => m.LoginName == "Joey");

// ... or use this syntax, which is equivalent after compilation
IQueryable<Member> query2 = from m in membersTable
                            where m.LoginName == "Joey"
                            select m;

// [3] Now execute the query
IList<Member> results = query1.ToList();
```

After step [1], you have an object of type `System.Data.Linq.Table<Member>`, implementing `IQueryable<Member>`. The `Table<Member>` class handles various SQL-related concerns such as connections, transactions, and the like, but more importantly, it holds a lambda expression object, which at this stage is just a `ConstantExpression` pointing to itself (`membersTable`).

During step [2], you're calling not Enumerable.Where() (i.e., the .Where() extension method that operates on an IEnumerable), but instead you're calling Queryable.Where() (i.e., the .Where() extension method that operates on an IQueryable). That's because membersTable implements IQueryable, which takes priority over IEnumerable. Even though the syntax is identical, it's a totally different extension method and it behaves totally differently. What Queryable.Where() does is take the existing lambda expression (currently just a ConstantExpression) and create a new lambda expression: a hierarchy that describes both the previous lambda expression and the predicate expression you've supplied (i.e., m => m.LoginName == "Joey") (see Figure A-1).

**Figure A-1. The lambda expression tree after calling Where()**

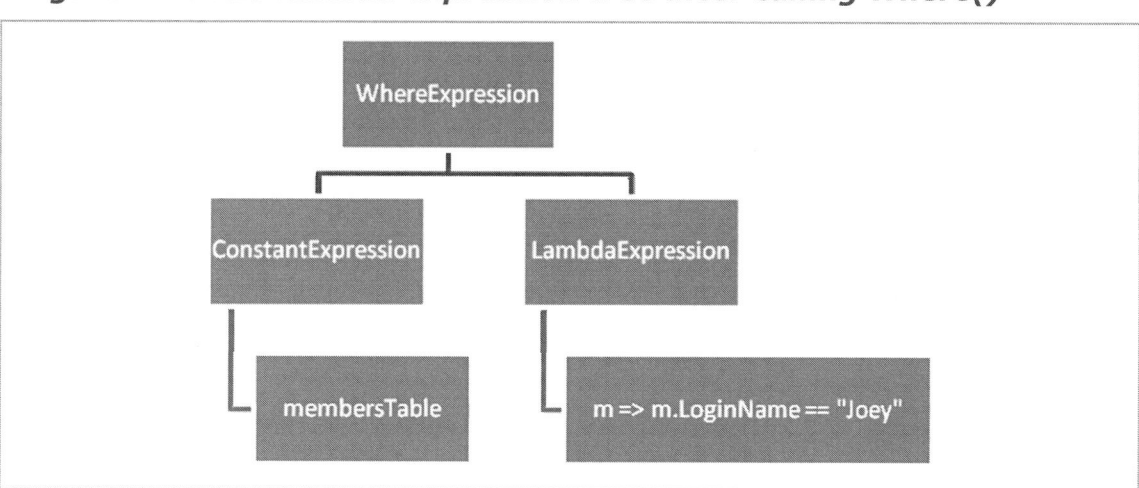

If you specified a more complex query, or if you built up a query in several stages by adding extra clauses, the same thing would happen. No databases are involved: each Queryable.* extension method just adds extra nodes to the internal lambda expression, combining it with any lambda expressions you supply as parameters.

Finally, in step [3], when you convert the IQueryable to a List or otherwise enumerate its contents, behind the scenes it walks over its internal lambda expression, recursively converting it into SQL syntax. This is far from simple: it has special-case code for every C# language operator you might have used in your lambda expressions, and even recognizes specific common function calls (e.g., `string.StartsWith()`) so it can "compile" the lambda expression hierarchy into as much pure SQL as possible. If your lambda expression involves things it can't represent as SQL (e.g., calls to custom C# functions), it has to figure out a way of querying the database without them, and then filtering or transforming the result set by calling your C# functions later. Despite all this complexity, it does an outstanding job of producing tidy SQL queries.

---

**Note**    LINQ to SQL also adds extra ORM facilities that aren't built on the `IQueryable<T>` query expression infrastructure, such as the ability to track the changes you make to any objects it returns and then commit those changes back to the database.

---

## LINQ to Everything

`IQueryable<T>` isn't just about LINQ to SQL. You can use the same query operators, and the same ability to build up lambda expression trees, to query other data sources. It might not be easy, but if you can interpret lambda expression trees in some other custom way, you can create your own "query provider." Other ORM projects are starting to add support for `IQueryable<T>` (e.g., LINQ to NHibernate), and there are emerging query providers for MySQL, LDAP data stores, RDF files, SharePoint, and so on. As an interesting aside, consider the elegance of LINQ to Amazon:

```
var mvcBooks = from book in new Amazon.BookSearch()
            where book.Title.Contains("ASP.NET MVC")
                && (book.Price < 49.95)
                && (book.Condition == BookCondition.New)
            select book;
```

# Related Titles

*Pro ASP.NET MVC Framework*, by Steven Sanderson (Apress, 2008)

*Expert Spring MVC and Web Flow*, by Seth Ladd et al. (Apress, 2006)

*Pro ASP.NET 3.5 in C# 2008, Second Edition*, by Matthew MacDonald and Mario Szpuszta (Apress, 2007)

*Pro LINQ: Language Integrated Query in C# 2008*, by Joseph C. Rattz, Jr. (Apress, 2007)

*LINQ for Visual C# 2008*, by Fabio Claudio Ferracchiati (Apress, 2008)

*Pro LINQ Object Relational Mapping in C# 2008*, by Vijay P. Mehta (Apress, 2008)

# Copyright

ASP.NET MVC Framework Preview

© 2008 by Steven Sanderson

ISBN-13 (electronic): 978-1-4302-1647-6

ISBN-13 (paperback): 978-1-4302-1646-9

Trademarked names may appear in this book. Rather than use a trademark symbol with every occurrence of a trademarked name, we use the names only in an editorial fashion and to the benefit of the trademark owner, with no intention of infringement of the trademark.

Distributed to the book trade in the United States by Springer-Verlag New York, Inc., 233 Spring Street, 6th Floor, New York, NY 10013, and outside the United States by Springer-Verlag GmbH & Co. KG, Tiergartenstr. 17, 69112 Heidelberg, Germany.

In the United States: phone 1-800-SPRINGER, fax 201-348-4505, e-mail orders@springer-ny.com, or visit http://www.springer-ny.com. Outside the United States: fax +49 6221 345229, e-mail orders@springer.de, or visit http://www.springer.de.

For information on translations, please contact Apress directly at 2855 Telegraph Ave, Suite 600, Berkeley, CA 94705. Phone 510-549-5930, fax 510-549-5939, e-mail info@apress.com, or visit http://www.apress.com.

The information in this book is distributed on an "as is" basis, without warranty. Although every precaution has been taken in the preparation of this work, neither the author(s) nor Apress shall have any liability to any person or entity with respect to any loss or damage caused or alleged to be caused directly or indirectly by the information contained in this work.